DREAM HOUSES ON THE WATER

ALEXANDER — HOSCH

Schiffer Publishing Ltd.

4880 Lower Valley Road • Atglen, PA 19310

Contents

WATERFRONT DREAM HOUSES

A few years ago, a story about dream houses that went horribly wrong was all over the media.[1] Famous people such as William Randolph Hearst and Madonna had disastrous experiences building their private dream homes. There is a precedent for this phenomenon: Nicolas Fouquet, the finance minister of the French Sun King, ended up in jail in 1661 after the envious Louis XIV hired Fouquet's master builders to create Versailles Castle. However, the last sentence of the article on dream houses instructed: start building tomorrow! This is how myths go, and the myth of the dream house is very much alive. And yet there are many positive stories, too. Sir David Chipperfield knew exactly how and where he wanted to build: in Northern Spain, right at the beach. His "House like Me" (page 16)[2] was built more than a decade ago. When Chipperfield recounts dinners with twenty family members, friends, and colleagues, you get the impression that this man's vacation home fits him well. Not only does he arrive at the sea on vacation, he also arrives at himself.

Glamour villas, noble cabins, mental buildings, minimalist temples

This volume features another twenty-nine mostly European houses on the waterfront where architects and owners have, for the most part, done things right. Some of recent work is the most significant. All of the houses are one-of-a-kind, and like people, they have their own personalities. Some are innovative and experimental, while others follow simple design principles. Each has a well-thought-out relationship to the water, whether it is dramatic or discreet. The homes are sited along mountain lakes, rivers, on Atlantic beaches, and on a Norwegian cliff overlooking the fjord. Their design addresses climate, topography, and the challenges and opportunities of building on the waterfront. There are glamorous dream villas such as Antonella Rupp's house over Lake Constance (page 148), elegant huts such as Claesson Koivisto Rune's small wooden home on Kråkmora Holmar (page 96), hermetic buildings such as Daniel Libeskind's Atelier House on Mallorca (page 156), as well as minimalist temples like Bruno Erpicum's Casa AIBS on Ibiza (page 70).

1 ——

Villa Foscari, called La Malcontenta,
in Mira at the Brenta canal.

[1] Fading myths: "Das Traumhaus" ("The Dream House"), in: *Süddeutsche Zeitung*, Feuilleton, 21/22. January 2006.

[2] "Casa come sé" / "Hous e as Self," in: *Abitare* 425, 2003.

Why a waterfront home?

Beautiful waterfront houses are more fascinating than homes that merely enjoy an elevated location or grand view. And, of course, waterfront properties, and those with a water view, are the most expensive. Germany's Lake Chiem, Tegern, and Starnberg areas are not the only places where you have to pay a premium for a water view. In the US, building permit fees often depend on whether a property is one, two, or five blocks from the coast. The former Olympic arenas on the East London waterfront have helped to revalue these formerly abandoned zones, and the residential sector there is experiencing a boom.

2 + 3 ——
*The water garden
of the imperial villa
Katsura has a pavilion
for moon and tea
ceremonies.
The main building
Shingoten, built from
1642 to 1647, was the
emperor's summer
residence in Kyoto.*

2

3

Water calms and also energizes: In Europe the fountains of Baroque castles once represented the element in constant flow. One example of a waterfront house is the Villa Foscari (fig. 1) built even earlier during the Renaissance. The family who owned it had a doge, or transport boat, and kept it conveniently at the Benta canal from 1559–1560, where it was easily accessible from the lagoon city. "If you can place the villa at a river, it is rather convenient, as you can transport the crops at little cost to the city using boats," declared the architect Palladio[3] in *I quattro libri dell'architettura* (*The Four Books of Architecture*). "Furthermore, the river serves household purposes and also is of benefit to the animals, apart from the fact that it provides cooling during summer and a wonderful sight. The estate can be watered effectively, particularly the ornamental gardens and kitchen gardens that are the house's soul."

While Italy and Germany recognized the practicality of being close to the water, earlier cultures simply appreciated its contemplative aspects.

4 ——
*The drama of architecture
and water: Frank Lloyd
Wright's Fallingwater.*

[3] From Andrea Palladio: *I Quattro Libri dell'Architettura*, book II, chapter 12. first published in 1570. Quoted here from: Helge Claassen: *Palladio, Auf den Spuren einer Legende* (On the Tracks of a Legend), page 109, Dortmund, 1987.

5 + 6 ——

View of the façade of E. 1027 and its step-on roof and the bay of Roquebrune-Cap Martin.

5

6

Japanese water gardens around noble residences, such as the imperial villa Katsura (1615–1663), focused on mirroring, visual illusions, and acoustics. Bodies of water with boat moorings and the sights and sounds of jumping carp or tortoises plopping into the water[4] were an integral part of these houses dedicated to leisure, with music pavilions, tea houses, and pond terraces for moon and star gazing (figs. 2, 3). They provided important ideas for the visiting European architects of modernism[5] such as Bruno Taut, Walter Gropius, Le Corbusier, and others.

Today, many people in the west are searching for that eastern perspective. Their minds become calm in the presence of a river or ocean. The flowing and heaving movement of water is liberating. The Greek philospher Heraclitus captured this idea in the words *panta rei*, which means everything is changing.[6] The sense of possibility and change, the eternal dynamic, and the additional value of the sweeping views are priceless.

Still a model: Modernism's steamboat

Frank Lloyd Wright's Fallingwater (fig. 4) from 1937 is stacked vertically and horizontally into nature. It is practically suspended from the Bear Run waterfall and even today is a model for any dream house. Another classic example is located on the French Riviera. Between 1926 and 1929, the designer Eileen Gray built the Maison en Bord de Mer E.1027 (figs. 5, 6) for herself and her partner in Roquebrune-Cap-Martin. It sits like an oceanliner on the rocks overlooking the Mediterranean Sea and Monte Carlo. Eileen Gray used her home by the sea as a design lab. Accessory features of this rather understated vacation architecture include the furniture made from steel tubing, the "transatlantic" deck chair, and the custom-made lighting and carpets. It may or may not be coincidence that these clever, lightweight items that later became bestsellers as licensed products were created for an upscale house that was difficult to reach. At any rate, they are once again appreciated as a model of sustainability and simplicity after postmodernism's orgy of shapes. Perhaps we should adapt as the motto of this book Eileen Gray's poetic "Invitation to Travel,"[7] which she handlettered in the living room of her beloved house.

---

[4] See Arata Isozaki (publisher): *Katsura. Imperial Villa*, Milan, 2004.

[5] Ibid.

[6] In Greek, "everything flows"

[7] "Invitation au Voyage" read a ship map over the sofa of E.1027. Other inscriptions painted by Eileen Gray read "Vas-y, Tonton!" ("Go away, stupid," a request concerning your car) and, at the entrance, "Entrez lentement" (Enter slowly). See Peter Adam: *Eileen Gray – Leben und Werk* (Life and Work), Munich, 2009, page 99.

7 ——
The Villa Savoye (1928-1931)

The principles of classical modernism are present elsewhere on the water. The architecture firm Claesson Koivisto Rune (page 124) was inspired by Alvar Aalto's atelier in Munkkiniemi. At Casa AIBS (page 70), Bruno Erpicum exhibits Le Corbusier's long window (fig. 7). From afar, the villa's white facade appears as if someone had pushed the architectonics of Kasimir Malewitsch into the granite cliff of Ibiza.

Adalberto Libera's Casa Malaparte (fig.8) is Matteo Thun's favorite from the modernist era. Ever since it was built in 1938 for the writer Curzio Malaparte, it has nourished dreams. It is sited at the perfect spot: on a rocky promontory on the island of Capri, only 600 meters (197 feet) from Thun's weekend home (page 84). Based on it, the architect, born in Southern Tyrol, painted the facade of his residence red. Even though the Casa Malaparte was a fiasco during its construction phase,[8] the view of its majestic roof staircase mobilizes thousands every year to take a trip along the cliff coast. Countless yachts and boats change course in order to pass the rocky outcrop where the Casa Malaparte is located, as if it had just briefly anchored there.

The romantic view of the exterior: design and emotion

There were strong feelings involved when Delugan Meissl in Austria planned the House RT (page 30) years ago. The Viennese architects based their work on the flowing spatial concepts of California architect John Lautner. He had built the theatrical Arango House overlooking a bay in Mexico as well as a series of villas on the US West Coast that provide a view like that from an eagle's nest and were used in James Bond films.[9] Lautner, who grew up in the untouched landscape of Lake Superior in Michigan, once said, "Architecture is meant for people, and this has been forgotten."[10] He deeply admired the "endless variety of nature," which he had discovered as a twelve-year-old while rafting tree trunks for a block house across a lake. He later integrated this yearning into his vacation homes.

Roman Delugan remembers, "When we first visited the property for House RT we stood on this high plateau, a spruce forest behind us, toward the front an almost endless view of the faraway mountains, in front of them the city and the lake. So, I thought, this is where I want to be warmed by the wonderful sun—someone give me a deck chair! We will open our picnic basket and enjoy this view!"[11] Today the living room sofa stands where the Viennese architect had wished for a deck chair. The windows frame the lake view for the owners. It is those simple ideas that can characterize a dream home.

These two houses are united by their contemporary aesthetic and the idea that nature can permeate daily life in a romantic way. The avant garde projects by John Lautner in Acapulco in 1973 and Delugan

8 ——
The villa unceasingly entices: boats come to visit the rock of the Casa Malaparte on Capri all day long.

[8] See the depiction in Michael McDonough: *Malaparte. Ein Haus wie ich* (A House Like Me), Munich, 1999.

[9] See Barbara-Ann Campbell-Lange: *John Lautner*, Cologne, 1999, pages 7 and 142.

[10] Ibid., page 7, quoted at a conference held by Lautner on January 23, 1991, at the SCIArc, Los Angeles.

[11] Interview, Elke Delugan-Meissl, Roman Delugan, and Christoph Schweiger, with Alexander Hosch on June 27, 2006, in the Vienna office of DMAA (unpublished part).

9

10

9 ——

Model for the unbuilt Open House.

10 ——

Oscar Niemeyer's 1953 Casa das Canoas in Rio de Janeiro.

Oscar Niemeyer did not model the house with the curved roof, but he did model the pool. Wolf Prix assimilated his ideas for liberating a house's footprint at Villa S.

Meissl in 2006 inspired the elevation of architecture from good to exceptional with their emphasis on living in nature.

In the case of House RT, the landscape becomes part of the house (just as the penthouse of the architect couple who designed Ray 1, shown in fig. 18). All of the views come from the outside, whether hail, lightning, or snow. "There is yearning, strong emotion, and a sense of ease and total relaxation. No decoration can compete with the ambience of nature."[12]

The treasured silver stripe

House RT is one of several houses in this book that don't lie directly on the water. Although the lake is some distance away, its charm and the view that it attracts like a magnet determined the house's shape and design. Its relationship to the large body of water can even be felt at the atrium with its pool. A thin silver streak in the distance is sufficient to become a moment that determines everything else.

Hirner Riehl (page 50) also created their House F in the wetlands quite far away from the shore; it can be reached via a long pier. The lake shimmers enticingly between reeds and birch trees; its strong aura is always present. Sometimes everything is wet; the land is marshy or even flooded up to the terrace. Studio Granda (page 60) encountered a similar situation at the Greenland Sea. It would have been impossible to build closer to the water due to the predominant winds. However, the owner wanted to feel the fjord as a permanent reference when standing in her living room. Nature, with the glacier, island, lighthouse, and sea, determines all of the emotional parameters of wilderness existence in this part of Iceland.

New houses for fun, sports, and life

The vacation Villa S by Coop Himmelb(l)au (page 102) has the joy of life in its genes—if you listen carefully you can hear the waves from California and Brazil. Wolf Prix, one of the firm principals, was inspired by a design in Rio (fig. 10) by the master of curves, Oscar Niemeyer, that entirely removed the house's footprint beneath the curved roof.[13] He also took cues from houses that his firm once planned for California, a dream landscape where Coop Himmelb(l)au has another office. The Open House[14] (fig. 9) was the conceptual anchor of that series. Its living area is metaphorically conceived as landscape. "There is a mountain, a valley, a lake, and a desert,"[15] Prix explains. "We wanted large, open spaces that are settled by the residents. But we never built the Open House." The Villa S in Kärnten profited from that experiment. In the end, Coop Himmelb(l)au's first residential design was not built on the Pacific Coast but at Lake Millstätt (fig. 12).

Villa S follows a strict internal organization; however, toward the water it is more free-form: the owner got a terrace reaching into the lake, a pavilion, and a boat landing with a diving platform and outdoor bar. There's more: with the Villa S, the old topic of "Gesamtkunstwerk" (synthesis of the arts)

---

12 From: "Wer baut mit Gefühl?" ("Who is building with feeling?"), Roman Delugan in conversations with the author and four other architects, *Architectural Digest*, March 2005, page 51.

13 Interview between Alexander Hosch and Wolf Prix on July 5, 2006 in Millstatt, published in part in *Architectural Digest*, Nr. 10/2006, page 252. Prix did not want a curved shape in Millstatt but placed the gable roof onto a "table" of steel and concrete columns to liberate the footprint on the first floor.

14 Study with flexible spatial organization, presented in 1983 and later in 1988/89, planned for Malibu. The Open House was never built.

15 Interview between Alexander Hosch and Wolf Prix in October 2000 in Vienna, printed in: *Architectural Digest*, Nr. 1/2001, page 20.

11

12

arrives at the water anew. The architects designed many items for this weekend home, from the sofa to the deck chair to the cocktail glasses with predator-hide prints. Another fun domicile is the Big Bay Beach House in South Africa (page 36). Fuchs Wacker designed it for a family in Cape Town. The briefing made it clear from the start—work is done in Europe! Now the couple, who met at the beach while windsurfing, want to teach their four children how to stand on the cool boards and can watch the kitesurfers in front of Table Mountain during the evenings.

The overhanging concrete house in Gerês (page 110) was also built because of the love of sports. The owners have been waterskiing in the river system of Northen Portugal for over twenty years. The wooden Casa Bouhon in Chile (page 130) was built for passionate windsurfers. And the beach house at Lake Starnberg (page 66) combines the owner's wish for a small and uncomplicated home with maximum freedom: as often as he wishes he can pursue his favorite pastimes of stand-up paddling and surfing, right from the terrace (fig. 11).

One elegant and trendy house floats rather than just standing there—Water Villa de Omval in Amsterdam, designed by +31 Architects (page 184).

Nature or sculpture?

One important decision precedes any construction project: how does the architect treat what he encounters on location? Does he respond to the drama of water and nature with submission? Or does he opt for orthogonal forms and colors that clearly show the human hand? There are many good reasons to have a building grow out of the environment in as simple a way as possible. For example, Matteo Thun strove to add as little architecture as possible to the surroundings for his conversion on Capri (page 84). His now overgrown house is hidden in the hillside. Lacaton Vassal (page 168) chose a radical variation for a new architecture by the sea: the firm designed a low-budget home on the French Atlantic coast that features pine trees and barely touches the ground. It can be about playing with the jungle or with saltwater, rocky cliffs, and marshlands—about prospect and refuge. Fantastic Norway (page 24) positioned a vacation home under a bionic protective shell on a rocky outcrop between the fjord and the sea so that the owners are never exposed to the winter storms, yet they have a fantastic view of them. Studio Granada cleverly flirted with eccentricity and imitating nature at the Greenland Sea (page 60).

Some of the newer small homes, such as the Beach House fitted into the contour of a fishing hut, are part of a different and often overlooked modern tradition: that of the simple cabin. Ever since Henry David Thoreau (1817–1862) wrote his essays on living simply with nature, the retreat in wild nature is seen as the place of the truly free. The American nature philosopher and dropout lived out his civil disobedience in a cabin close to Concord, Massachusetts, which was, of course, next to a small lake. "In such a day, in September or October, Walden is a perfect forest mirror, set round with stones as precious to my eye as if fewer or rarer. Nothing so fair, so pure, and at the same time so large, as a lake, perchance, lies on the surface of the earth. Sky water. It needs no fence. Nations come and go without defiling it. It is a mirror which no stone can crack, whose quicksilver will never wear off, whose gilding Nature continually repairs; no storms, no dust, can dim its surface ever fresh; a mirror in which all impurity presented to it sinks, swept and dusted by the sun's hazy brush—this the light dust-cloth—which retains no breath that is breathed on it, but sends its own to float as clouds high above its surface, and be reflected in its bosom still."[16]

11 ——

And another fun house: the terrace of the Beach House at Lake Starnberg invites activities.

12 ——

The land where cactus and oblique towers bloom: Coop Himmelb(l)aus's glamorous Villa S, in Kärnten.

One more look at Maison E.1027: it was the house that Le Corbusier would have liked to build, at a spot he would have liked to discover. As a guest he dipped his toes into Eileen Gray's pool as often as possible. During summer he lived on the terrace of the Bar Etoile next door, and later he occupied E.1027 with his planning staff, manically surrounded it with his own buildings; without Eileen knowing it, he added eight wall frescos to its interior.[17] In 1952 he caught cabin fever and erected his "Castle of 3.66 × 3.66 meters" (39 × 39 feet) next to E.1027. From this moment on, Le Cabanon (figs. 13, 14, 15) housed the noble savage. Le Corbusier built his manifesto on "living with sun, air, greenery" as a minimalist module—and until the end of his life he enjoyed the primitive cabin the most, including the diving platform that was built for him down by the ocean.

Why was this intellectual spirit so obsessed with this simple location? Perhaps because this perfect spot made the design almost effortless: the truly precious things are provided for free: nature, water, the expanse, the view. In Roquebrune-Cap-Martin, the living machine capitulated when faced with romanticism and nature.

A more recent Scandinavian example (page 96) provides a similar simple and comfortable living environment. Mårten Claesson, Eero Koivisto, and Ola Rune followed the principle of a

paradisical wood cabin on a small archipelago that blends with nature. By using generous terraces and clever proportions and optimizing the terrain, the architects fit a veritable vacation dream that leaves no wish unfulfilled on 45 square meters (484 square feet). Thoreau's ideal of autonomy and closeness to nature continues in time.

But Claesson Koivisto Rune has other options up its sleeve. The firm's 2010 residence close to Stockholm (page 124) is a pure white sculptural gesture. The angular design follows the Drevviken Sea like a mathematical figure. Bembé Dellinger, too, renounced local architectural poses on several new buildings in Upper Bavaria, such as the abstract Twin Home at the Amper (page 144).

The large-format home of Antonella Rupp overlooking Lake Constance (page 148) self-confidently features a tower consisting of interlaced chamois-colored cubes and places itself at the center of the landscape. The minimalist garden reinforces the impression of the house as a sculpture.

13

14

15

13, 14, 15 ———

The small wooden cabin, Le Cabanon at the French Riviera, became Le Corbusier's quarters in the Garden of Eden. At top left, the naked architect having a meal at the neighboring bar L'Étoile de Mer. Fantastic views and citrus trees flank the pathway between the cabin and bar.

[16] from H. D. Thoreau: *Walden*. The American original was published in Boston in 1854.

[17] See the comments by Peter Adam in his Eileen Gray biographies; also, texts by Peter Adam: "Haus der Eitelkeiten" ("House of Vanities") in: *Architectural Digest* 3/2001, page 88, and Alexander Hosch: "Mein Haus, meine Bucht, mein Sprungbrett!" ("My House, my Bay, my Diving Board!") in: *Süddeutsche Zeitung*, Feuilleton, September 8, 2003.

Welcome to the age of quality: from the Un-Private House to the Villa Careless

In 1999 the New York Museum of Modern Art organized the important exhibition *The Un-Private House*.[18] It presented photos, drawings, and models of twenty-six new or planned residences from all over the world. The radical presentation showed designs by Shigeru Ban, MVRDV, and Diller Scofidio as well as Rem Koolhaas's House in Bordeaux with its open office designed as an elevator that moves between three floors for the owner who uses a wheelchair. The MoMA exhibit presented a domestic lifestyle that seemed driven by a hunger for being on display.

That is hardly the focus today. Instead, architects work on eliminating the last minor inconveniences in the owner's routine. Rational and emotional considerations provide the impulse for decisions. For example, Barkow Leibinger designed a Berlin lake property (page 92) that combines studies in facade materiality with light-filled, high rooms and continuous views of the lake through a glass wall.

This dichotomy of openness and closure, combined with spectacular surfaces, has established itself as a model for waterfront properties. Schwarz & Schwarz (page 44) and Darlington Meier (page 180) experiment with a bronze skin on a house close to Zurich. At Lake Geneva (page 56), Kaufmann Widrig designs a provocative steel shell. Petra Gipp (page 162) separates the light-filled living cube on an archipelago from the wooden frame system for the bedrooms. Wespi de Meuron at Lake

Maggiore (page 116) and Bedaux de Brouwer in Zeeland (page 134) strive for maximum contrast between transparency and protection: here, coarse walls with boulders; there, ceramic clinker punctuated only by shooting window slits.

Steven Holl, on the other hand, uses thin wood framing and an angular deconstructivist pool to paint the interiors with soft, warm light at the Writing with Light House on Long Island (page 120) and the Daeyang Residence (page 78), respectively. And on Mallorca, Libeskind did exactly what the client wished for in order to be able to paint and sculpt to her heart's content: he resisted inflating the wonderful views. There is exactly one view of the ocean from the villa (page 156): less is more. Functionality after 2000 also means that architect and client do agree with each other. And they don't care about what other people think.

18 ——
The Delugan Meissl couple first tried out the shiny cover of glass and Alucobond at their own Vienna penthouse Ray 1. The two-level design over a 1960s block mediates like a membrane between the home and cityscape.

16, 17 ——
Günther Domenig in front of one of the turrets of his stone home. He built it after making drawings of stone formations in the Möll Valley.

[18] Exhibition at the Museum of Modern Art, July 1 — November 5, 1999, New York.

A few words about the progenitor of this type of well-built deconstructivist villa are appropriate at this point. In 1986 Günther Domenig tackled his own home at Lake Ossiach (fig. 17). The architect from Graz invented a canon of forms that anticipated the star creations of famous colleagues. The sculptural building that took him twenty-three years to complete appears unapproachable and confusing to some, even evil—a villa with staircase towers and pathways that lead nowhere. However, it is dream-like. Based on drawings of stone (fig. 16) that Domenig made during a sentimental journey to his favorite mountains of his youth,[19] he searched for and found his mystical home in bizarre steel turrets and concrete capsules. For many years he summered in the stone house.

19

20

19 + 20 ——
In 2009, Claesson Koivisto Rune custom-fitted a sailing yacht in Spain. At the steps of the stern we encounter the design's two most important ingredients: minimalism and walnut wood.

Efficiency, smart materials—and architects who build for themselves

Across the stylistic differences, the architects featured here have one thing in common: they are elegant problem solvers who delight their clients with efficiency and comfort. One variation is the architect who first tries out structural designs and materials for himself. His own home is a guinea pig, an eternal prototype that is permanently exposed to the possibility of failure, and a continuous work in progress.

Antonella Rupp tested fabrics, colors, and interiors for herself. Delugan Meissl tested the light metal Alucobond metal panels on their own penthouse first before applying it to House RT (fig. 18), which sits on the roof of a block from the 1960s like a paralyzed silver muscle. The architecture curator Terence Riley of the Museum of Modern Art in New York was reminded of a tattoo[20] when he saw the experimental exterior skin. Bart Lootsma compared the transparent structure with an X-ray image. [21]

John Pawson does not interrupt the view toward the water landscapes of his current creations with door handles, electric outlets, or lamps, and like Antonio Citterio (page 138), another residential specialist, he often tests details and clever solutions on his own house. David Chipperfield, who tries to see "the exceptional in the commonplace," illustrates the ideas of contemporary classicism with his vacation home by the beach (page 16).

The villa as a laboratory: "Small is more radical,"[22] adds Bolle Tham. He and partner Martin Videgård developed several motifs of the small Archipelago House (page 174) for use in large projects.[23] Like others presented in this book,[24] they dedicated their attention to the high-quality kit house—perhaps a trend. This allows them to pass on their discoveries to many others. Tham Videgård might be paradigmatic for the generation currently building.

---

[19] After thirty-five years in his native Möll valley, Domenig climbed the alpine pastures once again and drew the bizarre rock formations of the high mountains. From these "architectural demolitions," as he called these sketches, he built the structure of the Stone House.

[20] Terence Riley: Preface, page 11, in: Temel, Robert, Waechter-Boehm, Liesbeth: *Delugan Meissl 2, Concepts, Projects, Buildings*, Vol 1,
Zurich 2001: "More than most young firms, they have been able to maintain a vital element of experimentation in their projects."

[21] Bart Lootsma: *Röntgenarchitektur* (*X-ray Architecture*), page 15.

[22] See the profile "Nordlichter" ("Northern Lights"), page 62, of the architects in *Häuser* (*Houses*), August / September, 2012.

[23] "Central to their thinking was the conviction that architectural ideas are not really tested until they confront reality," page 6, in: Johan Linton: *Out of the Real. The Making of Architecture*. Tham & Videgård Arkitekter, Zurich, 2011.

[24] For example Matteo Thun and Claesson Koivisto Rune.

[25] See preface by Paula Antonelli: *Claesson Koivisto Rune Architecture/Design*, Basel, 2007.

The same is true of their compatriots Claesson Koivisto Rune (page 96), who want to be efficient above all. For example, this might mean furniture designed for the house. Claesson Koivisto Rune has contributed to the design of the new millenium, with regards to both architecture and design, said Paula Antonelli of MoMA[25] in 2007. Similar to Eileen Gray on the Mediterranean coast, the Swedish architects, which design for Iittala, Cappellini, and Boffi, practice aesthetic fine-tuning even for very small areas. The interior of a sailing yacht (figs. 19, 20) was fitted with a minimalist custom-made suit.

Outlook

Today's waterfront dream homes prove that feeling and emotion are back. People like to experience the elements and wish for smart materials, both inside and outside, that feel nice to the touch. And it is always about the right location: sometimes at the very bottom of a site, sometimes at the very top—but always sheltered from nature's forces.

Since the dot-com bubble burst in 2001, there has been a search for value rather than mere size. Downsizing and simplifying were ideas brought over from the US—and they stayed.

For this reason, today's expectations are not only measured in square meters or feet but in respect for nature. At the moment, luxury homes and Passive Houses are distant acquaintances. But who can say whether soon the homes in hot climates will get cool roofs that deflect heat and reduce the air conditioning load? Or that our next port cities will feature townhouse neighborhoods that use the nearby water to reduce energy, like larger buildings (fig. 21) are doing already?

One thing has not changed since E.1027, Casa Malaparte, and Le Cabanon: in the end, the client's emotional connection to a house and piece of land are more important for success than anything else. A house is a dream house not just when the guests admire it, but when its residents love it.

For all those who are currently only guests at waterfront dream homes, Eileen Gray's[26] sentiment applies: thumbing through this book should be like a voyage, full of discoveries, full of surprises!

21 ——

Will the next green wave bring energy-efficient town-house neighborhoods to new port cities? There are already deep wells on rivers that contribute to the heating and cooling of large residential tracts—as with the hospitals of BRT, built in 2011 in the Rheinauhafen of Cologne.

22 ——

Colorful boats next to Villa S in Millstatt.

[26] "Stepping into a home should be like a voyage, full of discoveries, full of sur- prises!" quoted in Peter Adam: "Haus der Eitelkeiten" (House of Vanities), in *Architectural Digest* 4 / 2001, page 90.

HOUSE IN CORRU-BEDO

SIR DAVID CHIPPERFIELD'S unique vacation home on the beach of a Galician village integrates the business hours of the firm's offices in four time zones with the leisure requirements of a star architect and his family.

BISKAYA —— 2002

Nature below, sculpture above: Chipperfield's vacation home "grows" out of the rocky beach.

The building in Northern Spain fits almost seamlessly into a row of fisherman's houses. It lies directly on the beach, at the edge of the eclectic string of houses facing the Atlantic. It grows out of the sea, out of the sand, out of the cliffs, like a stone, appearing as a contemporary-style monolith while sensitively echoing the symmetries of the village silhouette.

Every summer, the British architect David Chipperfield lives here with his family. When there are urgent projects to be discussed, Chipperfield's staff in London, Berlin, Milan, or Shanghai fly in. So far it is the only residence that Sir David Chipperfield has built for himself. With its grand simplicity, it contains everything that constitutes a good house.

"It is a wonderful place for spending the summer," he says. "We always stay for two months. The house has some 210 square meters [2,260 square feet], which is not that much, as I have four children. Its center is a large dining table and a sofa. There is no living room. The children's rooms are downstairs; farther up is a bedroom, conference room, office, and terrace. All summer long, people come to visit, and we accommodate them in the village. With the grandparents and the children's friends, there are always about twelve people around. We all meet here for dinner—that's about twenty people sitting at the table."[1]

This house is adaptive and yet has a distinctive identity, like the architect himself. This was observed—following a famous quote from Curzio Malaparte about his own villa on Capri—in a story about this project published in the Italian magazine *Abitare*.[2] It seems rather fitting.

Chipperfield, who succeeds in preserving architectural tradition without relying on dull imitation, realized his own minimalist classicism with this vacation home.

View from the loggia to the Atlantic coast and the boundary of a conservation area with dune vegetation.

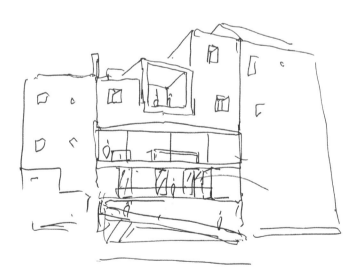

If the four-story building were standing in a city, one would not hesitate to call it a townhouse, as it is laid out like a city home. Yet it is innovative and atypical for its period. The access ramp from the beach is made from natural stone and cement, like the foundation. The main living level features a bank of sliding windows that take in the waterfront panorama and are the hinge of the design. The expanse of glass and the second-floor's pure white volume screening the loggia give the house a decidedly contemporary feel. The home's base and roof create a purposely unsettling nuance with respect to the surroundings. The capriccio effect of angles, fireplaces, and arches is a riff on the variety of gables on the neighboring houses and gently settles the younger home among them.

In the midst of Corrubedo's bustling environment, the hideaway invites strolls along the beach, swimming, and sailing, says Chipperfield, whose many honors have included being appointed as curator of the 2012 Vienna Architecture Biennale. His favorite activity is to simply sit at the glass front and gaze at the Atlantic.

[1] From an interview with the author in November 2005 in the London-Camden office, partially published in *Architectural Digest*, February 2006, page 48.
[2] "Casa come sé" ("House as Self"), *Abitare* 425, 2003, page 66: "If a house for yourself also means a house like yourself, one would be well-advised to look carefully at the holiday house David Chipperfield has just ..."

Fandango of rhythms:
the new white house is strikingly different from its neighbors,
yet it fits into the village silhouette.

SECTION

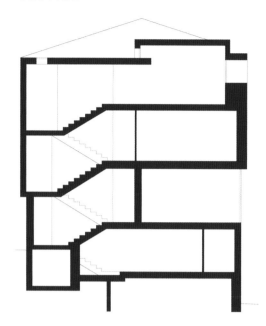

SITE PLAN

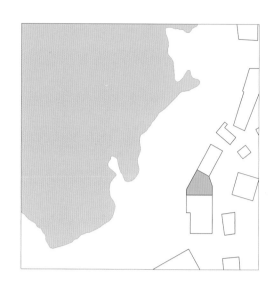

FIRST FLOOR/
BEACH LEVEL

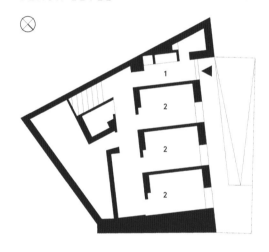

SECOND FLOOR

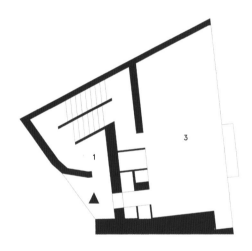

THIRD FLOOR

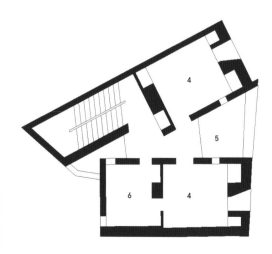

FOURTH FLOOR

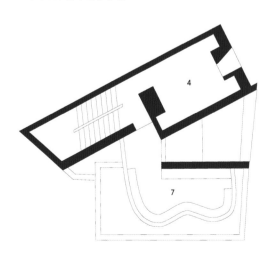

PROJECT DATA
David Chipperfield
Architects Ltd

Living area:
210 m² (2,260 ft²)

LEGEND
1 entrance
2 children
3 living/dining
4 bedroom
5 loggia
6 bathroom
7 terrace

The long dining table behind the illuminated glass front is the center of the home.
Bottom right: David Chipperfield in his vacation home.

"Family, colleagues, friends, and children—they all come to our home for dinner. There are sometimes twenty people sitting at the table."

DAVID CHIPPERFIELD ——

CABIN

FOSEN — 2008

VARDE-HAUGEN

A 360-degree view from the 35-meter (378-foot) cliff: the Oslo architecture firm FANTASTIC NORWAY explores the possibilities of building in an extreme climate with this weekend home between fjord and rocks.

"We strove for close contact between the landscape and inhabitants. There are things you cannot experience through maps and statistics."

HÅKON MATRE AASARØD ——

When you have panoramic windows and a wood stove, like the residents of this vacation home in Vardehaugen, you can enjoy the outdoors regardless of the weather. Despite whipping winds and snowstorms, the house is cozy inside. The architect Hakon Matre Aasarod designed the home for the site's wind conditions. "Every angle has been precisely calculated," he says. A senior partner in the Oslo firm Fantastic Norway, he built this 77-square-meter (828-square-foot) home for his parents, who live two hours away in Trondheim on the Fosen peninsula. The design process wasn't exactly a walk in the park given the exposed location between the fjord and rock ledge. To accommodate the extreme climate, Fantastic Norway reduced the structure to a formula: hard shell, soft core. The innovative roof wraps the house on all corners and down to the ground.

Matre Aasarod studied this site in central Norway to understand the views, the wind forces and direction, and the sun's angle in all seasons and times of day. "If I had only relied on local wind charts and statistics, the house would look different," he says. In addition to studying a regional dissertation about building on extreme sites, he performed tests with windsocks. The studies helped him to find the best niches for the terraces and design strategically placed edges and angles that outsmart the north wind.

The solid wood home is built directly on the rock (top).
To the left is a comfortable windowsill. With such a view of the fjord,
the weather is almost immaterial.

Black pine siding shields the home on all
corners and wraps down to the ground. The horizontal white
wooden battens are protected; the entrances and
terrace are also sheltered from the wind.

FIRST FLOOR

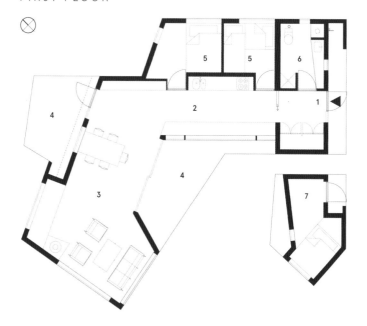

SITE PLAN

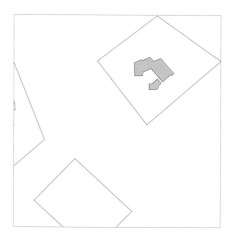

PROJECT DATA

Fantastic Norway AS
Håkon Matre Aasarød,
Sivilarkitekt MNAL

living area:
77 m² (828 ft²)

residents: 2

LEGEND

1 entry
2 kitchen
3 living
4 terrace
5 bedroom
6 bathroom
7 guests

SECTION

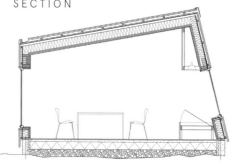

SECTION
The wood const-
ruction is rooted in
a concrete foun-
dation anchored
with steel columns.

A pendant light by
Paul Henningsen is suspended over the dining area.
To the right, the kitchen with a view of the protected
terrace; below, the living room.

HMA and his partner EBH had developed an intimate understanding of their country's building traditions during a three-year trip in a red motor home, which took them to sixteen Norwegian cities. They also drew on their experience designing a comfortable home 700 kilometers (435 miles) north of Oslo between rocky ground, mountain summits, and heathland with a view of the sea.

The home sits atop the rock, yet it seems to hunker down. The concrete foundation is anchored with steel pillars. The remaining construction consists of wood, including the roof. "The white lacquer of the protected horizontal wood battens contrasts with the black color of the vertical, elaborately impregnated pine cladding. This play of colors was a very important basic idea," the architect says. The footprint recalls the clustered buildings typical of Norwegian farmhouses, which are often placed so that a large building protects an ensemble of smaller buildings and creates an interior storm-protected patio. The house in Vardehaugen has only a small auxiliary building for guests, but the open-air space between them is sheltered from the wind.

The clients dreamed of a vacation home they could use as a nature observatory every weekend. Now they can watch eagles flying over the rocks and Hurtigruten ships passing on the Trondheim fjord. They can take walks in the mountains or take the boat out to fish for salmon, like the tourists do. It doesn't get dark during midsummer, and starting in autumn the northern lights make for dramatic night skies. It's easy to forget that the North Cape is still 1,500 kilometers (932 miles) away.

HOUSE RT

AUSTRIA —— 2005

<u>DELUGAN MEISSL</u> designed a contemporary atrium house with a lake view. From above, it might be mistaken for a crash-landed space-ship out of a *Star Trek* movie.

Green UFO: the green roof and artfully modeled landscape help the
home blend with its surroundings.

SECTION

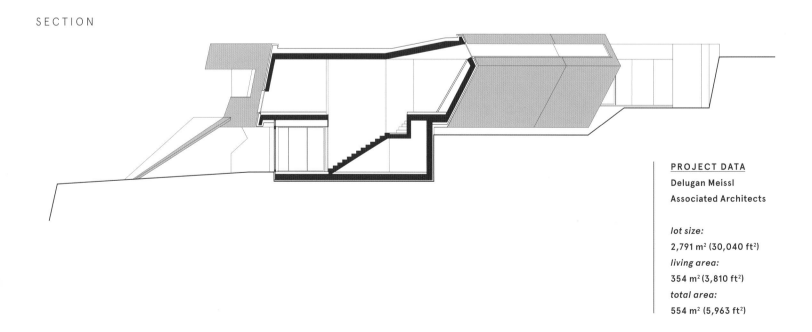

PROJECT DATA
Delugan Meissl
Associated Architects

lot size:
2,791 m² (30,040 ft²)
living area:
354 m² (3,810 ft²)
total area:
554 m² (5,963 ft²)

"From the living room you see the city and the lake. We framed this view with something like a passe-partout."

ROMAN DELUGAN ——

On the exterior, the wings and wedges appear rugged.
Inside, however, there is only harmony.
"Everything blends together," says Roman Delugan.
"The shapes contribute to the flow of space." The living room floor is
made of walnut. Armchairs in the atrium are by Patricia Urquiola.

One of the best single-family homes in the portfolio of Viennese architects Delugan Meissl is a villa in rural Austria that looks like an extraterrestrial vehicle. "The design sort of developed from the future living room," says Roman Delugan. "We were standing on the slope looking at the city, the mountains, and the lake, and we imagined what our clients would like to see when sitting on the sofa." To illustrate this point, he picks up a section drawing of House RT and indicates the living room cockpit.

This house embodies his design philosophy, as does his own, somewhat older Viennese penthouse named Ray 1[1] (fig. 18, page 12). Delugan says that the location and site dictated the house's form, rather than any preconceived idea about how it should look. "We developed it step by step with the clients," he says. The front of the house references the almost endless expanse of the lake. Built on a platform under a spruce forest, the house is nearly opaque on the side facing the trees, with only narrow bands of windows. "Little Red Riding Hood is part of the story—after all, there is something menacing and mysterious about a forest at night," he says. "Here you can feel secure and lean with your back toward the forest. It supports the house."[2]

Roman Delugan and Elke Delugan Meissl and their colleagues based the avant-garde residence on the idea of creating both flow and a secure sense of place. The interplay between house and landscape references American architect John Lautner's work in Mexico and California during 1960s and 1970s. "Like him, we work with emotion and create flowing transitions between the rooms and from nature into the house," Delugan says.

FIRST FLOOR

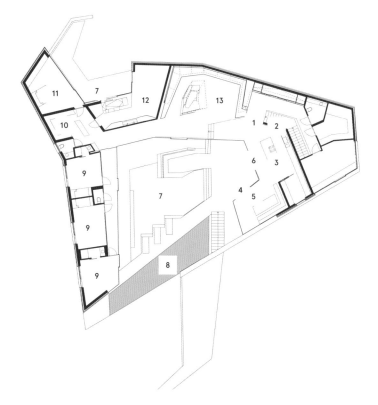

House RT appears to consist of a single level because its basement rooms are set into the hillside. The interplay between wild and domesticated nature and its relationship with the building was more important to the architects than the house's form. House and nature interlock at the front while remaining separate at the rear.

Delugan Meissl Associated Architects, who designed the film museum in Amsterdam and the Winter Festival Hall in Erl, are at their best when designing private residences. That's because they observe the "speed" of each client or family. Every room is assigned a "tempo." Right angles express stillness, as in the children's rooms. The more the angle is opened, the "faster" a room flows. "This is how little by little the custom-made suit for our client was created," Delugan says. "Only after looking twice do you see that you are dealing with a common typology: the atrium house." Exterior cladding consists of black Alucobond boards that protect the house like a tortoise shell. All of these elements combine to form an interplay of contrasts. "There is yin and yang, quietness and noise, light and dark," Delugan says.

"The nice thing about this house is that we could design everything, from the basement to the kitchen, fireplace, bench seats, and domesticated nature. It was complicated and elaborate, but it fits our idea of building," he adds. "For us there is no separation from one object to the next. Everything is made as if it were from one single cast. The architecture reacts to the owner and the landscape.

The atrium deck's Indonesian bangkirai wood withstands the tough alpine climate. On the left is the polygonal living room with Alcantara sofas and a central fireplace. Indirect illumination and speakers were integrated into the terrace.

Not just yin and yang, but high tech, too. The facade's scores are assymetrical and abstract: black Alucobond boards have wide, visible joints "like a black leaf in nature," says Roman Delugan. The bathroom behind it, with its bathtub set into the slate floor, is one of the house's most spectacular rooms.

This is the key to our houses." This holism is an essential characteristic of every Delugan Meissl residence. "The furniture is built into the spatial flow—you cannot change it like clothing." Over the lake in Austria, the hierarchy of architecture and furniture has been thoroughly dissolved.

[1] See *Architectural Digest* 2/2004, "Im Himmel über Wien" ("In Heaven over Vienna"), page 151, and "Bauwelt" ("Building World") 23/2003, page 10. The Ray 1 penthouse resulted in a sort of celebrity status for the architects because they interpreted the strict Viennese building code in a creative way. The dwelling appears as a two-story muscle with metal skin and seems to have been paralyzed in the middle of a twitch.

[2] See *Architectural Digest* 10/2006, Alexander Hosch "House RT," page 62. All further quotes are from a partially unpublished interview between Elke Delugan Meissl, Roman Delugan, and Christoph Schweiger with the author at their Viennese office in the summer of 2006.

BIG

BAY
BEACH
HOUSE

CAPE TOWN —— 2010

The Stuttgart firm **FUCHS WACKER ARCHITEKTEN** designed a private home for maximum vacation fun on one of the coolest surf beaches in South Africa.

Fynbos-covered dunes help to protect the house. Below, surfers are on view from November until June, and, with a little luck, even whales. Shown here is the passage between the main house and guest house near the pool.

You feel like you are on vacation every minute of the day

STEPHAN FUCHS ——

Robust exterior wood withstands the intense sun and extreme wind. The shutters are made from Canadian cedar, the decking from ipe.

In Cape Town the sun is in the north. This takes some getting used to, but visitors to this vacation home quickly adapt. The wide wooden terrace on the south has sweeping views of the nearby Bay of Cape Town. Table Mountain, South Africa's most well-known icon, keeps watch. On the west-facing front of the house, a protected strip of the typical fynbos dune vegetation separates the beach house from the breathtakingly wild and usually frigid ocean. On the east side, a wind-protected interior patio with pool beckons; the architects set it between a natural stone wall outside the two-story main house and a single-level guest house. The clients, a family with four children, live in Europe but visit Cape Town regularly. One of the owners grew up here, and it is no coincidence that the house is on the Big Bay—one of the best surfing spots, particularly for kitesurfing, as the couple met here while surfing. Fortunately, there are fewer sharks here than on Cape Town's east coast.

The owners and their architect, Stephan Fuchs, quickly agreed on a design. Fuchs is one of the two owners of the Stuttgart firm Fuchs Wacker and is himself a windsurfer. "Building on a waterfront is the most exciting project type by far," he says. "From dawn until sunset, you can see the surfers from the terrace." The house was literally built on sand. The 2.5-meter (8-foot)-deep steel columns secure the building to its foundation, which was filled with tightly compacted sand. In addition to the main building for six, the guest house offers room for four people.

The volumes respond to the unique geography and climate. "The building was influenced by the proximity of the water and the strong sunlight, and particularly the strong winds that blow continually," Fuchs says. "All of the exterior wood is durable, ages beautifully, and already has a nice, silvery shimmer.

The main house's first floor consists of a single, light-filled room where the entrance, kitchen, stove, dining area, and fireplace hall align. The open staircase is the central motif. It opens up views and manages light and shadow, like the many sliding doors, curtains, and wood panels. The residents can decide where they want the sun to warm them and where they want to feel cool. "The living area is entirely glazed on both sides so we can always see the ocean," Fuchs says. "Everything here gets wet, as the house is not far from the

Fynbos vegetation covers the dunes between the house and Atlantic.
The house is literally built on sand. The clients met at this site on the
beach, rather romantically: his dog, usually a loner, allowed her to
pet him while his master was riding the waves.

SECTION

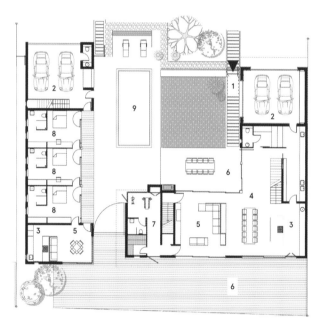

FIRST FLOOR

TOP FLOOR

SITE PLAN

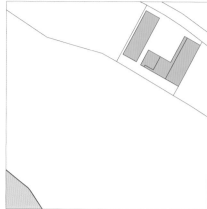

PROJECT DATA

Architekten BDA
Fuchs, Wacker
Stephan Fuchs,
Thomas Wacker

lot size:
1,900 m² (20,450 ft²)
living area:
350 m² (3,767 ft²)
additional area:
110 m² (1,184 ft²)
residents: 6+4
type of construction:
steel, concrete, and
masonry

LEGEND

1 entrance
2 garage
3 kitchen
4 dining
5 living
6 terrace
7 sauna
8 guests
9 pool
10 children
11 play area
12 bathroom
13 master bedroom
14 sun deck

dangerous Cape of Good Hope. We chose materials that contribute to the feeling of being at the beach, such as natural wood and stone. After all, you spend most of the time barefoot and wearing only swimming trunks, so it is important that the surfaces feel good." The terrace decking is made from ipe wood; shutters and facade cladding are untreated Canadian cedar. The polished natural stone floor consists of gray granite slabs that predominate in the Cape area. The reddish wood of the staircase, the dining table, and the oiled parquet floor boards is afromosia. Linear light apertures in the roof accent the corridors and bathrooms. A small sauna offers a fitting conclusion to long days of surfing when the ocean's temperature is only 12 degrees Celsius (53 degrees Fahrenheit) in summer.

From the fireplace hall, a separate staircase leads to the detached guest house, which consists of a large bedroom and bathroom. The top floor features an additional terrace overlooking the pool area. Viewed from the sea, the design resembles a clamp that is open at the top. This sculptural gesture gives the two buildings a cohesive appearance. From the beach, the houses look like a single building. The region's unique vegetation is part of the land's dramatic beauty. So when you ask about the best view, even the architect hesitates: "Waking up in the morning and watching the first surfers on the incoming waves?" Or perhaps "enjoying a sundowner on the terrace while the sun sinks into the sea."

The master bedroom looks out on one of the most beautiful views on earth. Below is the open living room.
In the background are kitesurfers and a view of the majestic Table Mountain.

TERRACE HOUSE
IN ZOLLIKON

ZÜRICHSEE —— 2010

With <u>**LUCAS SCHWARZ'S**</u> steel and concrete house for his brother Andreas, a lot that once held an old Swiss family home is catapulted into the present.

SECTION

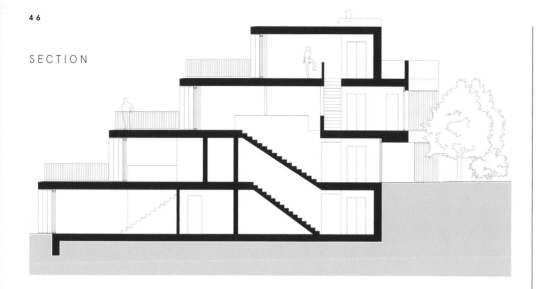

SITE PLAN

FIRST FLOOR

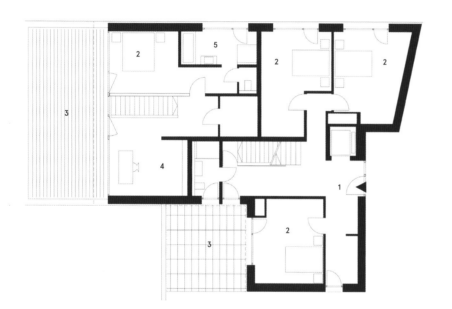

PROJECT DATA

Schwarz & Schwarz
Dipl. Architekten SIA

lot size:
842 m² (9,063 ft²)
living area:
300 m² (3,299 ft²) plus
guest area 130 m² (1,399 ft²)
additional area:
345 m² (3,714 ft²) plus
guest area 141 m² (1,518 ft²)
terraces:
120 m² (1,292 ft²) plus
guests 40 m² (431 ft²)
residents: 5
guest apartment: 3
energy concept:
certified MINERGIE®
standard, ventilated
facade with vertical
overlapping bronze
panels

LEGEND

1 entry
2 bedroom
3 terrace
4 office
5 bathroom
6 living
7 kitchen/dining

TOP FLOOR

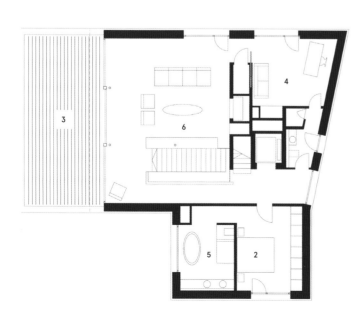

ATTIC

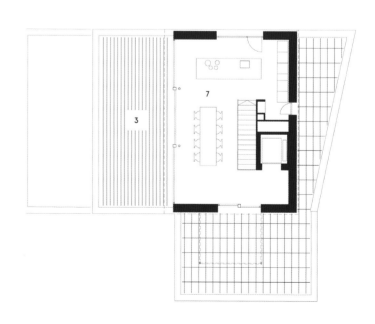

Heavy metal: at night the interplay between viewing and veiling is striking.
The kitchen at the top has an almost wraparound terrace.

The old house from 1920 on the so-called Gold Coast needed more than a facelift. So the owner decided to replace it with a terrace house. "The horizontal, stacked floors respond to the sloping hill location," says architect Lucas Schwarz about his design overlooking the northeast coast of Lake Zurich.

From the lake, however, the building looks like a glass cabinet. Generous sliding doors guarantee fantastic views of the lake from all four floors. The garden level houses a separate apartment, and the five family members share the three floors above. All of the floors feature spacious terraces or balconies with panoramic views of the lake, emphasizing the fact that the outdoor experience is primary here. "The staircase design puts the water view in the spotlight," the architect says. "It anchors the house and opens to a different experience of each floor."

The building's other striking feature is its cladding. Schwarz & Schwarz chose twisted vertical bronze metal sheets for three sides to provide contrast. The panels glow in the sunlight, adding brilliance and movement to the facade. Their shape varies in all directions in original ways. Lucas Schwarz describes it as an "active facade as opposed to the calm surface of the water."

Oak decking throughout the house provides a contrast to the bronze facade.

The burnished and patinaed bronze sheets were partially perforated with a laser—at the entrance, for example. The offset metal facades dissolve the massive masonry and concrete walls with their blade-shaped assembly and horizontal arrangement. In 1946, Richard Neutra finished his Kaufmann House with similarly elegant aluminum blinds. The architect and owner, who works in the designer furniture industry, put much thought into this metal curtain. The press promptly proclaimed the new building in Zollikon "unique," at least for Switzerland. [1]

[1] See "Bronze-Zeit" ("Bronze Age") in: *Atrium*, November/December 2011, page 50.

Metal fins are perforated at select places.

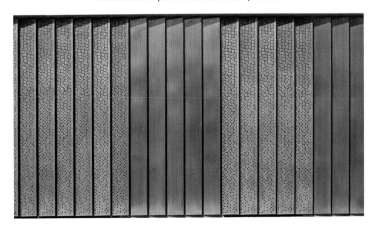

HOUSE F

WÖRTHSEE —— 2007

This marshland near a lake close to Munich called for a lightly built house with pile foundations. The house, by the Munich office of **HIRNER** and **RIEHL**, elegantly "floats" between the birch trees as if it were a raft. Sometimes the water reaches the edge of the terrace.

When the marshland floods, the house seems to float between the birch trees like a large raft.

The light-flooded stairwell is enhanced with skylights,
see-though staircase risers, and "flying treads."

You sit inside the house, and yet in nature.

This house sits on the western shore of Lake Wörth in Upper Bavaria opposite a small island, and abuts a nature reserve. An artist couple divides their time between it and their city apartment. Marshland conditions dictated that the house be built as lightly as possible. Positioned between the water and firm ground, it rests on piles inserted deep into the earth and columns 60 centimeters (2 feet) in diameter. Architect Martin Riehl conceived the house as a raft clad in prefabricated wood panels, with an oak jetty stretching about 100 meters (328 feet) to the water.

Wood, a classic boat-building material, also binds CO_2 and its choice was part of the firm's determination to build sustainably. Some of the exterior surfaces facing the garden are clad in wood veneer. The rest of the facade features horizontal larch boards over a frame of super-strong cumaru wood. Next to the main building, a garage and studio are also clad in larch, and interiors are partially covered in white plaster.

Riehl is particularly pleased about two aspects: "That the house, minimally invasive, has become a link between the shore and the water. And that the owner enjoys living there." Riehl points to a bench at the water's edge, reached via the jetty through marshland. From there one gazes back toward the house shimmering between a scrim of birch trees and reeds, and out toward the catamarans on the lake. The small jetty offers private access to Lake Wörth. For some time now, a catfish has been living under it, recounts the owner with a smile. The architect sits next to her and points out a bird house whose flat, slanted roof echoes that of the house.

The relationship between nature and building is palpable. "This place in particular allows us to experience how architecture reflects the geographic characteristics of a place," Riehl says. Design team members Martin Hirner and Matthias Marscher note the interplay between open and closed areas. Toward the north the building has no windows. Facing east, only a high window slot is visible on both floors. The living area provides vertical views and the top floor is illuminated by skylights. To the south and west the house opens into the landscape. Here the skylight glass can be removed for dining in the midst of nature.

This spot has become a natural idyll with a catfish in residence under the boat landing and clouds on the lake.

FIRST FLOOR

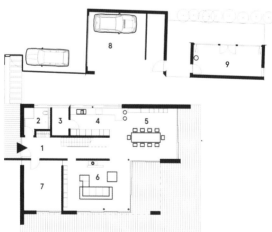

TOP FLOOR

PROJECT DATA

Hirner & Riehl Architekten und Stadtplaner BDA

lot size:
2,914 m² (31,370 ft²)
living area:
364 m²/283 m² (3,918 ft²/3,046 ft²)

LEGEND
1 entry
2 bathroom
3 technical
4 kitchen
5 dining
6 living
7 office
8 garage
9 atelier
10 bedroom
11 sauna
12 dressing area

SITE PLAN

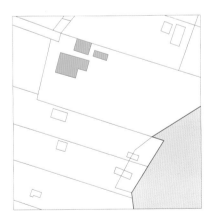

SECTION

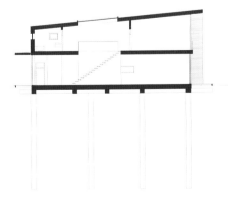

On stilts:
60-centimeter
(2-foot)-thick
columns anchor the
home in the 12- to
20-meter (40- to
66-foot)-deep gravel
layer. In between are
loess and clay strata.

View across the property toward the lake. The second-floor deck is made of
cumaru wood, and the skylight opens for additional breezes.
One of the clients made the sculpture.

STEEL HOUSE

KAUFMANN WIDRIG ARCHITEKTEN
from Zurich set a new residence into
the fruit orchard of an old park villa. Its
facade will change from black to rust-
colored over time.

LAKE GENEVA —— 2009

AT

THONON

SECTION

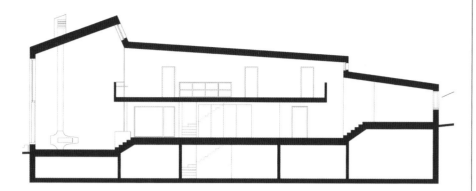

FIRST FLOOR

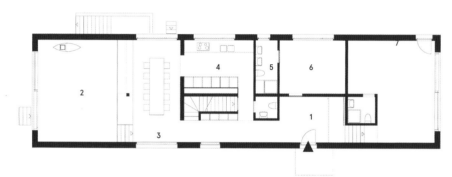

SECOND FLOOR

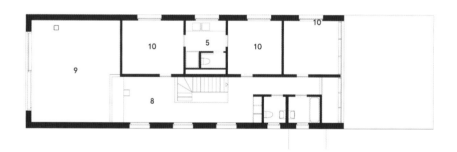

SITE PLAN

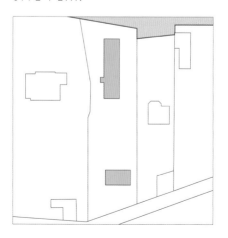

PROJECT DATA	LEGEND
Kaufmann Widrig	1 entrance
Architekten GmbH	2 living
	3 dining
lot size:	4 kitchen
2,000 m² (21,530 ft²)	5 bathroom
living area:	6 guests
305 m² (3,283 ft²)	7 studio
lower level:	8 gallery/office
540 m² (5,813 ft²)	9 airspace
technology:	10 bedroom
heat pump	

"The client wanted a rational yet personal lake house," says architect Daniel Kaufmann. He and his business partner had worked for the experimental Zurich firm Gigon/Guyer and are used to exploring limits.

The property is long and narrow. "Next to the existing villas, our house looks like an annex," Kaufmann says. The new residence prefers to blend with the boat houses next door. It sits at the very front of the lot, directly at the shoreline, commingling with the dark wooden huts with gable roofs that open their doors for all kinds of boats. They belong to the whitewashed hillside villas centered on their respective lots.

Kaufmann Widrig Architekten not only matched the design and geometry of the neighboring buildings, but they reiterated the constuction type and materials, too. "The outer steel skin and the wooden interior remind us of ship architecture," Kaufmann says. "They are also an abstract reference to the boat houses." Inside, walls and ceilings are clad with larch boards that complement the landscape and rust-colored facade, and the floors are made of polished concrete.

Top: the gravel area under the plane tree next to the house is the architect's
favorite place. The owner likes to look out from the larch wood interior
of his living room, watching the arriving and departing ships (left).
Opposite: a study of the steel facade.

The house is in Thonon, on the southern French shore of Lake Leman,
not far from Evian. The view is to the north through the 5.5 meter
(18-foot)-high windows of the two-level living room. The dining area,
kitchen, open corridors, and an office on the gallery connect to the
living area, with its ceiling up to 8.3 meters (27 feet) high. This way the
available space is utilized in its entire length and height. The owner
can watch the ships berthing and putting out to sea at the neighboring
pier. When sitting at his desk on the gallery he also takes advantage of
the extra-large, four-panel windows facing the lake.

The architects choose black steel plates for the facade; the material
is more affordable than Corten steel. They will develop a saturated
red rust layer over the next thirty years and contrast with the blue-
green of the garden, lake, and sky. "The unusual material and its
purposeful aging are perfect for this project," Kaufmann says. "In
addition, we wanted to design the roof from the same material, which
was possible with steel plates."

Rooms are stacked toward the rear and contain angled skylights that
scoop southern light into the interior. The rusty-red villa contains 305
square meters (3,283 square feet) of living space, plus a lower level
housing a sauna and another studio. Outside, a gravel terrace under
pollarded plane trees has become a favorite place to sit.

HOUSE AT THE

In Iceland, **STUDIO GRANDA** designed a comfortable family home in a harsh environment.

GREENLAND SEA

SAUÐAKROKUR —— 2008

Architect Steve Christer took the basalt for the floors directly from the site. "Basalt columns are a tourist attraction in Iceland," he says. "First we had the stone cut in Reykjavik. Then we brought back the slabs and built them into the house." The living room looks out on the sea.

"Perfect happiness? To sit on the windowsill and watch how the midnight sun dances on the ocean."

STEVE CHRISTER ——

The house at the end of the island is part ranch, part villa. Twice a week a small plane flies from Reykjavik to the northern wilderness at the Greenland Sea. This meant that architect Steve Christer, who runs Iceland's most prominent architecture firm with his wife Margrét Hardardóttir in the capital city, was stranded high in the north more than once due to storms and snow. "Even for an architect from Reykjavik, the Greenland Sea is a very remote building site!" he says.

An Englishman, Christer studied at the London Architectural Association and spent three years building this wooden house in Hof for a family of five who found Reykjavik too congested. Building here was a challenge, but an interesting one, Christer says. "Iceland's architecture does not have as many traditions as other places do. This is good on one hand and bad on the other. It requires the architect to make all decisions himself, rather than looking to history or tradition." Nature's forces reign in Iceland's unpopulated central regions—lava fields, volcanos, waterfalls, and geysers—and here on the northern coast you encounter colorful houses, small lakes, treeless pastures, long table mountains, and a huge fjord.

Architect and client Liljja Pálmadóttir, an artist, found a common response to this extreme setting: simplicity. Christer embedded the house in a wall-like enclosure and oriented the rooms to the views. The scenery is pristine when the dense fog dissipates! During winter this place at the polar circle is completely dark and the temperature falls to minus 20 degrees Celsius (minus 4 degrees Fahrenheit). In these moments, mysticism and magic, dreams of evil trolls or heavenly fairies are not far away.

The floorplan is oriented around several landmarks: the volcanic Drangey and Málmey Islands, the sparkling Arctic Sea, and the Unadalurjökull glacier. An old sheep shed and the lighthouse provide points of reference. And 500 meters (1,640 feet) away is the equestrian paradise. From the kitchen you can always see the paddock, stable, and new riding hall. Not only is the barn an object of passion, it is also a daily workplace. The owner's Icelandic horses are intelligent, beautiful, strong, and tough—just like the home.

Stone slabs run from inside to outside. The exposed-concrete corridor
is illuminated by small skylights.

Due to the peat walls that are reminiscent of old Icelandic
farmhouses, the home appears as if it were buried. Rooftop plantings further embed the architecture.

SECTION

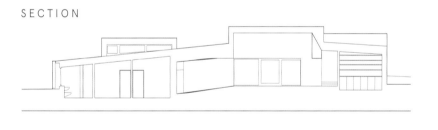

FIRST FLOOR

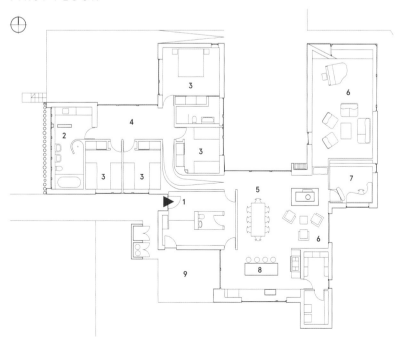

PROJECT DATA

Studio Granda Architects

lot size:
50.8 ha (126 acres)
living area:
294 m² (3,165 ft²)
residents: 5
energy concept:
Passive House, highly insulated, geothermal system

LEGEND

1 entrance
2 bathroom
3 bedroom
4 playroom
5 dining
6 living
7 office
8 kitchen
9 terrace

It took Studio Granda many years of work to wrestle this residence from nature. "Even more than elsewhere, on Iceland you build with the wind and the sun," he says. "You can't fight against them." Outdoor space on the fjord side of the patio is barely usable. The wind from the prairie is too strong and reaches every nook and cranny. "There are veritable tornados here, and the roof withstands extreme conditions," Christer says.

The bathroom is fitted with polished basalt slabs consisting of hardened lava.
Walls are clad in marble tiles. Below is the kitchen.
Above, owner Liljja Pálmadóttir with her cattle dog Bingo.

Most of the material was shipped in—a long process—because Iceland has neither a concrete nor timber industy. The oak roof beams came from England. Only Alaskan poplar and birch trees can grow roots in Iceland, and unprotected tree plantations are eaten by sheep. Wood for the windows, tables, and built-in furniture was imported, as were the beige-gray cedar boards for the exterior. The silver-colored boards and the grass on the roof help to hide the house in the landscape. Peat walls, which recall old Icelandic farmhouses, also help to embed the architecture in nature.

The owner wanted the house to age like her grandparents' old farmhouse. The facade's wood surfaces are either flat, three-dimensional, or curved. Black basalt floors, exposed concrete, and weathered wood are a foil for the owner's colorful interiors. "I couldn't live with sterile elegance," says the owner, who paints and makes sculptures and reliefs that are sensual, organic, and often amorphic.

The home's careful detailing is best expressed in the basalt slabs that cover most of the floors. Their original hexagonal shape was preserved. Slim basalt columns are a sightseeing attraction in Iceland, says Christer: "We took the stone from the excavated construction site, brought it to the capital to cut it, and then transported it back." A talented craftsman then laid the stone pattern that recalls the body of a gigantic snake.

The remoteness of the Arctic Ocean and the polar circle can be perfectly enjoyable—if you have a house that matches your personality, and when you are busy around the clock with children, nature, and horses.

LAKE STARNBERG —— 2008

BEACH HOUSE

Fishing cabins offer the opportunity to mediate between tradition and the present. Design firms **TILL BOODEVAAR** and **ARNOLD WERNER** discovered the potential for a relaxed beach house in the redesign of a small wooden house.

SECTION

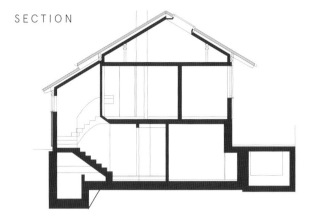

FIRST FLOOR

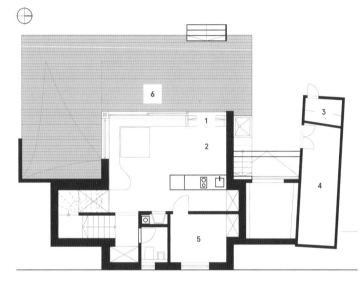

SITE PLAN

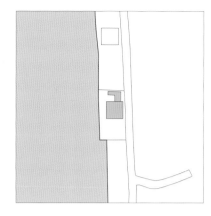

TOP FLOOR

PROJECT DATA
Arnold / Werner
Sascha Arnold,
Steffen Werner

lot size:
ca. 250 m² (2,691 ft²)
living area:
75 m² /40 m² (807 ft²/431 ft²)
residents: 1–2
energy concept:
fireplace on two levels

LEGEND
1 entrance
2 living/kitchen
3 sauna
4 storage
5 guests
6 terrace
7 evening living room
8 bedroom
9 dressing area
10 bathroom

Chilling out, lounging, living: some 75 square meters (803 square feet) of living area at the water are sufficient for the young entrepreneur because they are perfectly designed for his sporty life. The elegantly paneled rear wall on the first floor hides the bed, bathroom, and dressing area.

View toward the south. The grill in the background is rarely cold.
Below, the terrace deck with the owner's sports toys.

Classic fishing cabins have a distinct waterfront typology. In 2008, a new residence replaced a 100-year-old derelict home on the eastern shore of Lake Starnberg. It had to fit precisely into the old footprint. The result is a 75-square-meter (807-square-foot) lifestyle oasis that serves as the launching point for sports activities.

Architect Till Boodevaar was bold enough to confront tradition while adhering to local building codes. He set the wood home in concrete like a white trough on a layer of gravel. The first floor consists of steel and concrete, while the top floor is clad in cedar. The deck was built with ipe wood, and the window frames, interior built-in furniture, and flooring are teak.

Inside and out, the home was fitted for its intended use as a beach house. The side facing the street is inconspicuous; pedestrians notice only the ornate nineteenth-century villas on the other side on the hill.

The architect was instructed to open up the beach house to the lake with large glass walls on both levels. The living room level on the first floor and the bedroom level upstairs consist of one large room, each with a terrace. Sascha Arnold and Steffen Werner, of the firm Arnold Werner, fulfilled their client's wish to build in as much of the furniture as possible. The first floor's paneled rear wall is part of a cleverly designed guest room that integrates storage space, a sleeping bunk, dressing room, and bath. Teak parquet floors feature black joint filler typical of boat floors. The refrigerator, TV, and storage container are on wheels so that everything can be rolled and neatly stored away, and the kitchen has a stowaway work surface. The living area is big enough to accommodate tables and comfortable seating for work, chilling out, and lounging. Large windows of 4 to 6 square meters (43 to 64 square feet) can be opened, lending a feeling of being on the beach.

"Many times I swim in the lake early in the morning and then drive to work with wet hair. What a start to the day!"

THE OWNER ——

A passionate windsurfer, water-skier, and pioneer of stand-up paddling, the owner can enjoy his water sports and a view of the Zugspitze Mountain. Next to the main house is another small shack with a mini-sauna and storage space for the surf boards. The owner uses the out-door grill almost daily and hardly needs his kitchen during the summer. The same is true for the bathroom—from April to October he showers outdoors.

IBIZA —— 2004

CASA AIBS

BRUNO ERPICUM
set classical modern and contemporary architectural features into the scenic aura of a Mediterranean house on a cliff. The result is a veritable zenith.

My private Ibiza: the definition of drama is living 159 meters
(522 feet) above the Mediterranean Sea.

Bruno Erpicum's houses are large, cool, brilliant white, and pay homage to modernism. Many of them are in Belgium, but about fifteen are on Ibiza, including Casa AIBS. It sits atop a granite cliff on the northern coast, 159 meters (522 feet) above the Mediterranean Sea. The interplay with the landscape makes it one of the most exciting compositions by the Brussels-based architect and his Atelier d'Architecture.

The flat-roof residence is closer to Richard Neutra or Le Corbusier than to the local rugged farmhouses. Swimming pools, reflecting pools, and shallow ponds line the long orthogonal building. The most intriguing elements are the glass walls that dematerialize next to a pool or pond.

One particularly successful design feature is the infinity pool: it captures the setting sun if you are sitting at the right spot. Here, nature is your neighbor. Lying in the bedroom's lounge chair, you can look out on the scenery as if it were a stadium seat: the pool, the rocks, the Mediterranean hillside vegetation. From here it all appears to fall into the ocean.

"I like it best when architecture is the sole decoration," says the minimalist Erpicum. He structures buildings as rooms that are endlessly long or rise high in the air. White walls sit in the landscape without enclosing anything. Light slits and apertures define and dramatize the sun's movement. Kitchen, beds, cabinets, and doors were custom-made by the local artisan Gregorio. The built-in furniture is block-like and monolithic, just like the architecture. Only the light-brown wood has a soft, warm appearance. Hard edges are softened, however, by the client's collection of furniture and figural sculptures.

At Casa AIBS, Bruno Erpicum was inspired by Le Corbusier.

Bruno Erpicum is convinced that a location creates its own ideal building. You only have to allow it to do so. Shown here is the master bedroom with slate slab flooring.

"The first thing I do is listen.
The lot tells me how it wants
the villa to be."

BRUNO ERPICUM ——

FIRST FLOOR

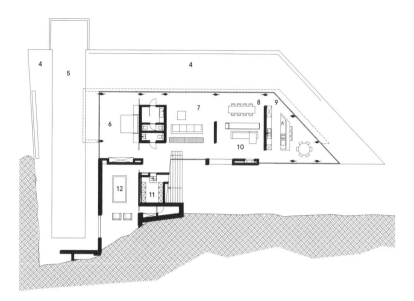

TOP FLOOR

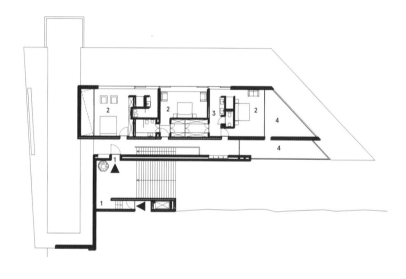

SECTION

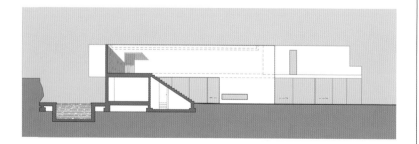

PROJECT DATA

Atelier d'Architecture
Bruno Erpicum & Partners

lot size:
2,000 m² (21,530 ft²)
living area:
450 m² (4,844 ft²)
additional space:
250 m² (2,691 ft²)
residents: 6

LEGEND

1 entrance
2 suite
3 bathroom
4 terrace
5 pool
6 bedroom
7 living room
8 dining
9 kitchen
10 fireplace
11 utility room
12 billiard/home cinema

The real value of the Casa is found in its surroundings: it is a house without neighbors, integrated into the rocks, both an invitation and high art. How to hide the conduits and foundation? How to integrate the lighting and the facade? How to transition from this jagged environment to a human-scaled living environment?

In this case, it is accomplished with steps to the house along a natural pathway lined with steep cliffs. Inside the home, the steps simply continue. Erpicum plants patches of lavender on the terraces and pine trees on interior patios. At one point his design frames an olive tree on the cliff, which acts as a stone wall for the patio.

Interior sight lines emerge out of the strictly organized volumes. The layout is reminiscent of the geometries of Kasimir Malewitsch and the plasticity of De Stijl. Other elements reference Le Corbusier, such as the long window (fig. 7, page 8). The bedroom level behind it rests on slim piers.

Erpicum convincingly interlaces these motifs of classical modernism with architectural minimalism, such as the facade framing and the panoramic window.

SITE PLAN

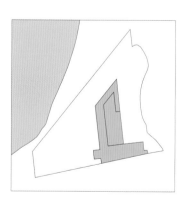

Vistas and vertical windows accentuate the large living area. In the background is the dining area and kitchen.

DAEYANG RESIDENCE AND GALLERY

SEOUL — 2012

The sound of light and colors: musical sketches guided architect <u>STEVEN HOLL</u>'s design for an experimental gallery residence in the hills of South Korea. A pool amplifies its flickering light and shadows.

Upper-level interiors are wrapped in reddish bamboo.
Below, architecture that makes a point.

In the hills above Seoul, Steven Holl designed a private residence with a lower-level art gallery. A large pool dominates the new residence and functions as an axis for light reflecting into the gallery and onto the walls of the upper living cubes. The client's program called for three pavilions for receptions, living, and events.

The surrounding pool lends a sense of weightlessness to the substantial cubes, built on an exposed concrete foundation. Commissioned by the Daeyang Shipping Company, this experimental design was executed along with the research project "The Architectonics of Music." Holl based the building's geometries on a sketch by Istvan Anhalt, who composed "Symphony of Modules" in 1967, that Holl found in a book by John Cage.

Building proportions are based on the numbers 3, 5, 8, 13, 21, 34, 55—the so-called Fibonacci series. With a theme of rooms activated by light, the pavilions' flat roofs were fitted with fifty-five long, linear skylights. The skylight slots, along with artificial light bounced off the surrounding water, result in a choreography of light that changes from season to season and day to day, and the continuous flickering enlivens the building ensemble.

This project underscores Holl's reputation for bringing together physics and poetry. The organizational structure is simply an instrument for the improvisational play of water and light. The "reflecting pools" amplify the effect of the cutouts and act as a kind of impressionistic counterdraft to the rational architecture. Small glass lenses in the bottom of the pools cast reflections on the white granite floors and the gallery walls below, lending the ambience of an aquarium. Upper-level interiors, including the walls, floors, and ceilings, are wrapped in red bamboo, and the exterior is clad in copper.

Water is visible everywhere. "Visitors open a door, go up a flight of stairs, and arrive at a bamboo wall inside the entrance patio," Holl says. "From this central location they can see the three pavilions as they seem to drift away on their own light reflections." Unfortunately, jumping in for a swim, however inviting, is not part of the plan.

The musician John Cage would have liked the design's many light effects.
Above is a Steven Holl watercolor of the living pavilion.
Below is the event area.

FIRST FLOOR

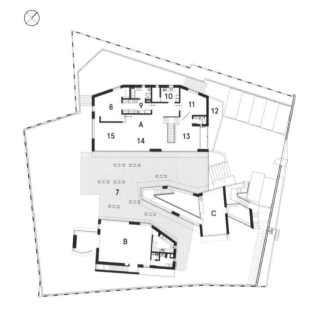

SECTION

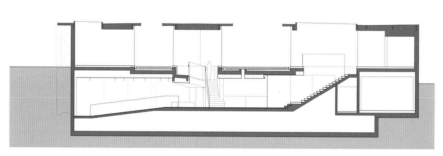

LOWER LEVEL

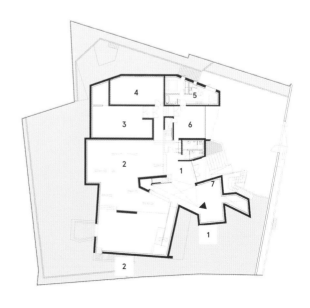

LEGEND

A residence
B event area
C reception

1 entrance
2 gallery
3 atelier
4 technical
5 janitor residence
6 garage
7 water
8 bedroom
9 dressing room
10 kitchen
11 bedroom/library
12 terrace
13 conference room
14 dining
15 living

PROJECT DATA

Steven Holl Architects

lot size:
1,760 m² (18,940 ft²)
area:
994 m² (10,700 ft²)
residents: 2

Ascent from the gallery to the reception pavilion. On the opposite page is another sketch.

CASA

CAPRI —— 2008

THUN

Almost every weekend, <u>MATTEO THUN</u> flees from the "factory" that is Milan. During winter the architect meets his family in the Engadine mountains; in summer they decamp to the Tyrrenian Sea and their wonderful house on the island of Capri.

The guest house glows in red, just like the Casa Malaparte a few hundred yards away.

Overgrowth of civilization as a concept: Casa Thun is invisible from the ocean.
Bougainvilla and other plants (below) grow over facades and pergola. Above, the pool.
The chestnut ladder leads to a comfortable open-air seat.

The conversion of the old farmhouse on Capri, fifteen minutes and 150 steps away from the nearest street, was no small challenge for Matteo Thun. There is no real opportunity here to build efficiently. This is because any building material must be carried up on someone's shoulders. "This circumstance obliged me, my wife Susanne, and my two adult sons to limit the renovation and furnishings as much as possible," he says. What does this mean? "Only the essentials are here—things you need for eating, sleeping, and sitting. Even my drawing paper is reduced to a minimum."

The gradual ascent to the house is rewarded by a grand view over the bay of Marina Piccola to the south of Capri. To the left, the famous Faraglioni rocks protrude from the ocean; to the right is a comfortable perch from which to observe the boats and yachts that move around busily all day. The stable, cistern, and chicken shed were converted into a living room and bedroom. Railings, ladders, and the pergola frame are made from chestnut wood, as is the custom on Capri. It has to be replaced every ten years. The floor consists of light-colored natural stone. "There are really no great ideas here," Thun says with understatement, "apart from the fact that each family member has a bedroom facing the ocean and a bathroom facing the mountain. And then there is the common living room, which also faces the sea."

PROJECT DATA
Matteo Thun & Partners

lot size:
1 ha (2.5 acres)
*living area (main build-
ing):*
220 m^2 (2,368 ft^2)
residents: 4
energy concept:
solar energy for house
and pool

Just do nothing!
Susanne and Matteo Thun have enough work to do
when in Milan. Weekends on Capri they hang loose. At
bottom right, the terrace in front of the guest house.
The tiles come from the Amalfi coast.
To the left, the owner's watercolor paintings depict his
home and surroundings.

Nevetheless, this two-level Capriote farmhouse has been turned into a contemporary residence, a Matteo Thun house. A large steel beam was added for support. Next to the home, an infinity pool beckons. The nearby outcrop is one of Thun's favorite spots: this is where he does Pilates in the morning. A staircase follows along the left side of the house; next to it is a modest guest house. Its color is rosso pompejano—like the famous Casa Malaparte (fig. 8, page 8) a few hundred yards away on a rock protruding from the sea. Casa Malaparte is Thun's favorite modernist residence. "The only things I don't like on this island are the bright white neo-Capriote buildings," he says. "I reject this so-called Capri style. There are only a few fantastic old farmhouses here, and they are usually whitewashed. But a house like this should remain invisible. We wanted to hide it. If you look up from the sea you can barely make it out. And that was the intention."

This was accomplished by planting lush vegetation including bougainvilla, citrus trees, wisteria, and jasmine. A boccia court sits between the agaves and cactus. Between the garden gate and the entrance of the house, the aroma of herbs such as lavender and rosemary fill the air.

Hence the Thuns are busier as gardeners than as designers when they are on Capri. They like to spread out on one of the terraces: on the flat roof, in the dining area, under the pergola, on the pool terrace, or next to the colorful Amalfi tiles on the guest house. Thun grows nostalgic when his sons climb the limestone cliffs behind the house or practice free-climbing over the water. "This spot is similar to the dolomite in my homeland of South Tyrolia where I first practiced climbing," he says.

The casa is subordinate to nature on all levels. The most important questions were: where do I place a table so it receives sunlight in the morning and shadow in the afternoon? Where do I plant the bougainvillas, and what color should they be? Where is the best sunlight for a cactus and where is it best for an olive tree? "None of these are classic architectural criteria," laughs Susanne Thun. "Our home on Capri is comparable to a bivouac box on a glacier," adds her husband. "You can only have the essentials." Simplicity indeed.

Matteo Thun wanted to add as little architecture as possible to the existing house. Life is comfortable nonetheless. Each family member has a room facing the ocean and a bathroom facing the mountain. Below, the large living room with a floor made of pietra serena di Val Malenco (porcelain stoneware). The Baroque mirror is Neapolitan, and the white wooden chairs are originals from Chiavari.

"My favorite place here is everywhere."

MATTEO THUN ——

"This house was sited perfectly," says Matteo Thun.
"Not 10 yards over the ocean, where it is humid, and not 500 yards
higher where it would be almost impossible to carry up things."
This is the view from the pergola to the boats in front of the Marina
Piccola. In July the bougainvilla sports purple blooms.

VILLA

BERLIN —— 2007

AT LAKE OBER

BARKOW LEIBINGER ARCHITEKTEN experimented with materials in this shiny metallic cube on the shore of a small Berlin lake. It is situated close to the Lemke country home designed by Mies van der Rohe.

Building without disturbing:
the villa by Barkow Leibinger confidently and considerately
fits into its heterogenous environment.
The brickwork facade of Mies van der Rohe's countryside home
Lemke can be glimpsed on the left.

SECTION

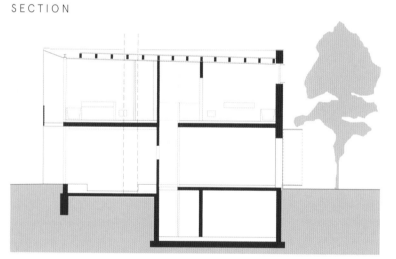

SITE PLAN

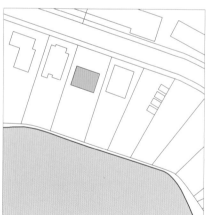

PROJECT DATA
Barkow Leibinger
Architekten

lot size:
1,157 m² (12,450 ft²)
living area:
264 m²/313 m² (2,842
ft²/3,369 ft²)
residents: 1
energy concept:
KfW 60, geothermal
heat, photovoltaics

LEGEND
1 entrance
2 bedroom
3 living
4 dining
5 storage
6 office
7 cinema
8 guests
9 children

FIRST FLOOR

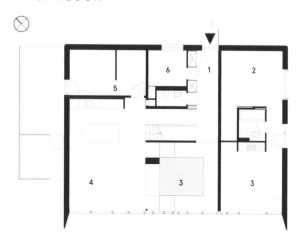

TOP FLOOR

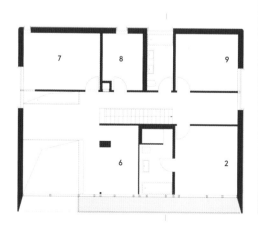

Glittering: silvered mosaic tiles clad the street facade.
Below, the dominant fireplace in the open living room, which looks out on the lake.

Large square windows guide the lateral views away from the dense neighborhood and toward the lakeshore. The southern facade, on the other hand, consists solely of windows and all the rooms face Lake Ober. Two-level access, along with terraces and balconies, create airy, flowing transitions between the living area and garden.

The client uses his flat-roof home for living, to entertain guests, and as a work studio. The large living area is double height, and a fireplace and seating corner connect the dining area and kitchen. The library on the gallery is also part of this perceived unity. Bedrooms are upstairs and face the lake or the street. Family and friends use the guest apartment. The narrow hillside lot was empty when the owner purchased it. Next to it stands a home that dates to the original colony of villas. The lake was created in 1895 as a water reservoir for a brewery. Mies van der Rohe's 1932 Lemke villa, an L-shaped bungalow, is two houses away. The venerable neighborhood prompted the ambitious architect to experiment with materials for this formally rather inconspicuous house. In addition to the silvery facade, entrances and the carport were fitted with folded steel canopies. The window frames of the insulated brickwork construction are made from larch wood, the roof consists of wood shingles, and the balcony railing is an industrial fence.

It has been called "perhaps the most exciting house in Alt-Hohenschönhausen."[1] Berlin architects Frank Barkow and Regine Leibinger designed the villa for a German film director. He can jog around a lake at three in the morning all by himself, he has said, and it is only twelve minutes away from the Alexanderplatz.[2] The silvery, shimmering waterfront home of over 300 square meters (1,027 square feet) was a successful surprise in this diverse neighborhood that brings together Gründerzeit villas, relics of the Soviet occupation, and East German industrialized apartment blocks.

The architects say that the starting point for their design was the distinctly different environments on the property's four sides. The northern street facade is closed and allows for only partial views. Here the windows are hatch-like or ribbon-like; north, east, and west facades are covered with round, silver mosaic tiles that reflect the sky, trees, and water.

[1] See "Das ist Berlin" ("This is Berlin"), in: *Berliner Morgenpost*, February 11, 2008.
[2] Ibid.

ORNÖ — 2003

VACATION HOME ON KRÅKMORA HOLMAR

Simplicity and elegance combine in the hideaway on a small island of Stockholm Schärengarten.
CLAESSON KOIVISTO RUNE opened up three sides of the glass and wood building toward the Baltic Sea. The fourth facade facing the higher-lying adjacent home was closed off.

Simply beautiful: 45 square meters (484 square feet) on the
ocean are sufficient for a family's desire for freedom.
Exterior materials include spruce, glass, and galvanized steel.

A young family commissioned Claesson Koivisto Rune to build a summer home on the Baltic Sea. It lies on a small island, only four meters (13 feet) from the water on a rocky hillside and next to a small brook. The interior is narrow like a corridor and oriented lengthwise, with a bend between the living room and bedrooms. Essentially a large cabin, the design is an interplay of possibilities, contrasts, and the romanticism of the simple life. Large-format views of the ocean make the house feel larger than it is.

"We were inspired by the geometry of the granite rock on which the house rests," says architect Mårten Claesson. Following the Ice-Age topography, the design is slightly angled at the waterline. This determined the other forms, such as the hybrid roof covered with tar paper shingles. The building combines the aesthetic elements of a monopitch roof with a conventional saddle roof. The wing with the highest ceiling contains the living room and kitchen and is crowned by a saddle roof. Its gable line continues with the bedrooms at the longer side. "This made it possible to design a saddle roof with diagonal gables, which is rather unusual," Claesson says. A small house on Kråkmora Holmar in front of Ornö was the first of a series of folded-roof houses by the Stockholm architects, though they follow a slightly different geometric principle.

The clever angles avoid a block-like appearance and make the house appear larger. Its simple exterior combines natural-looking materials such as silvery spruce on the siding and deck and galvanized metal panels below the windows and doors.

Terraces with steel wire railing open the vacation home to the outdoors. Above, the view from the bedrooms.

The house is opaque toward higher-lying neighbors eight meters (26 feet) away. The 45 square meters (484 square feet) of living area are complemented by a large terrace facing the ocean. Its elevated location allows for a view across the rocks into the spruce treetops. The wood construction rests on a poured concrete slab supported by columns and secured with steel cables along the terrace floor boards. A sunbathing platform sits a bit farther away.

SECTION

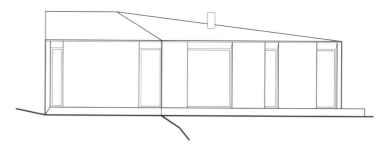

FLOOR PLAN

PROJECT DATA
Claesson Koivisto Rune
Arkitektkontor AB

living area:
45 m^2 (484 ft^2)
residents: 5

<u>LEGEND</u>
1 entrance
2 storage
3 bedroom
4 living
5 kitchen
6 terrace
7 bathroom

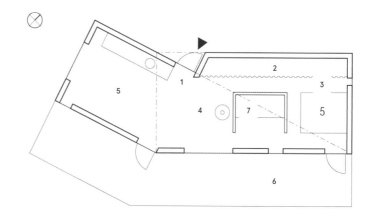

The facade follows the topography of the granite rock. The stove (left) is the only heat source .
The wall behind it separates the kitchen from the bedrooms.

VILLA S

Learning from Malibu:
COOP HIMMELB(L)AU,
which has been operating a
branch office in
Los Angeles for twenty
years, built its first
vacation villa in Carinthia.

LAKE MILLSTÄTT —— 2006

"If I build something like this, I have to feel comfortable myself. And I would move in right away!"

WOLF PRIX ———

It is hard to believe, but this lake pavilion in Millstatt was shaped by local building codes. Constraint became a virtue. And a conversation turned into an inventive project. This was the first private home commission for the Viennese architecture firm Coop Himmelb(l)au. There was almost no space left to build on this narrow parcel, but by constructing a large platform that juts over the lake, the clients gained additional living space. The pavilion is accessed via a corridor and staircase and consists of aromatic cedar decking and four folding glass windows that open to cool the interior on hot days. The owner likes to nap here or use it as a jumping off point to the lake.

Carinthia has almost Mediterranean conditions; palm and olive trees can winter outdoors. Small open pavilions are common in Austria and along Lake Millstatt. "A fantastic climate! Why should we build as if it were Norway?" says Wolf Prix, one of the firm's founders. "Upstairs we had to slightly compress the rooms, but on the first floor we simply opened the house to free up the floor plan."

The pavilion's central motif is a leaning tower—the firm's trademark—that contains a sculptural blue steel staircase. Says Prix: "This vertical element is decisive for the design; its obliqueness is central to the dynamics."

Careful, just by pushing a button, a wine rack might pop up from the basement! The architects wrestled the white terrace with a staircase and a jetty from the lake. Eye-catching:
the oblique tower and the cedar pavilion are shown opposite left.

Architecture and design
by Coop Himmelb(l)au: concrete table, acrylic chair,
and the living room sofa "Mosku" are only some of the
exclusive designs for the owners. Artist Peter Koglerhe
developed the curtain pattern.

California Dreaming in Carinthia:
jacuzzi, diving platform, century-old olive tree.
The owner stores watersports toys under the deck floor.

A central motif of the Villa S, both inside and outside: the blue-silver staircase tower.

SECTION

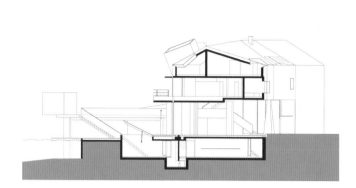

SITE PLAN

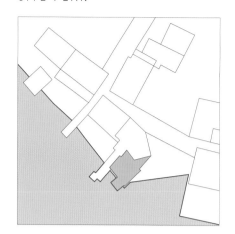

FIRST FLOOR

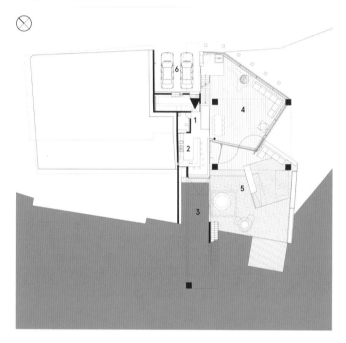

SECOND FLOOR

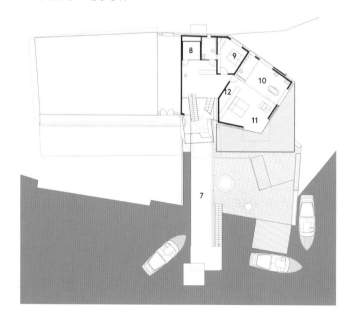

THIRD FLOOR

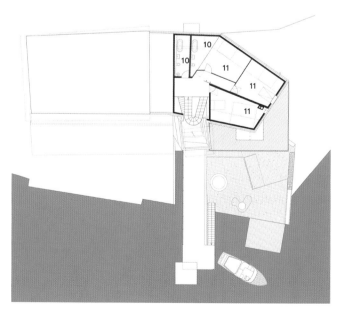

Where is Malibu again?
The motorboat above is anchored in
Carinthia next to the kitchen bar.
To the left, one of the views from a neighboring lot
toward the villa with its canted tower.

PROJECT DATA

Coop Himmelb(l)au
Wolf D. Prix
& Partner ZT GmbH,
Dreibholz & Partner ZT
GmbH
living/outdoor area:
500.46 m²/787.42 m²
(5,387 ft²/8,476 ft²)

LEGEND

1 entrance
2 kitchen
3 boat house
4 living/dining
5 terrace
6 garage
7 gangway
8 sauna
9 guests
10 bathroom
11 bedroom
12 dressing room

This gesture allowed the basic idea to be realized: the upper quarters maintain a formal look with the slanting roof, as though they were placed "onto a table," Prix says. It also made possible an open floor plan below with space for the entrance, living room, kitchen, and bar.

The pavilion's beauty also lies in its many details: a terrace with white planks and a 100-year-old Sicilian olive tree, a diving platform, a boat jetty that reaches out into the lake, and a rope hoist located almost inside the kitchen. Here the vacationing owners can enjoy a drink after a boat outing or an afternoon of angling.

The house is filled with custom pieces designed for the family of three children and their guests, including a wine rack, bench, concrete table, acrylic chairs, sun lounger with wheels, leather sofas, plates, and cocktail glasses. Other pieces were made by well-known Austrian artists such as Peter Kogler, Erwin Wurm, and Eva Schlegel.

Only after careful consideration did Coop Himmelb(l)au give in to his client's wish for a white house. With it, the noted architects added a sublime villa to their collection of shimmering metal clouds, elegant glass cylinders, and twisted concrete towers.

In Portugal, **GRAÇA CORREIA** and **ROBERTO RAGAZZI** designed a dramatically cantilevered concrete house with a river view.

CASA NO GERÊS

CANIÇADA —— 2006

This vacation home is located in Peneda Gerês National Park not far from Guimaraês, Portugal's first capital city established in 1140. The site's trees could not be cut down, and the Cavado River that runs through the nature preserve had to be protected as well. The clients, a water-sports-loving couple with one child, were drawn to this region of rivers and reservoirs and requested that the house be closely connected to the river. Correia Ragazzi Arquitectos designed a 150-square-meter (1,614-square-foot) house with an exposed concrete facade that protrudes over the hillside. Beneath it, the land slopes toward the river. The Portguese architects also repurposed a ruin next to it as a guest suite.

"From the very first visit to the building location, we knew we were dealing with a delicate and special project," Correia and Ragazzi said. The architects modeled the home after the landscape effect of the Casa Malaparte on Capri (page 8) and the table "Less," designed in 1994 by Jean Nouvel for Molteni. The single-level, orthogonal building has ceiling-height windows on three sides that allow the greenery to permeate. It is a skewed prism defined by six pairs of congruent par-allelograms. While the building exterior is under-stated, the interior is finished with light-colored birch. The center area contains the entrance and kitchen. The bedrooms are located next to the rock wall, the dining area floats over the river, and the roof can be walked on. Flooring consists of self-leveling gray concrete screed.

The adjacent guest house, the former ruin, is acc-essed via a steep gravel path, while the pathway to the main house is a skewed staircase made of large, square-cut stones. A shower, bathroom, and storage space for sports gear occupy a small building set apart from the main house.

Living over the river: experiencing nature without disturbing it.

Dramatic protrusion: the concrete fireplace wall was inspired by a table made by Jean Nouvel.

PROJECT DATA
Correia / Ragazzi Archi-
tectos
Graça Correia,
Roberto Ragazzi

lot size:
ca. 4,060 m² (43,700 ft²)
living area:
150 m² (1,615 ft²)

LEGEND
1 entrance
2 dining
3 kitchen
4 living
5 bathroom
6 bedroom
7 guests

SECTION

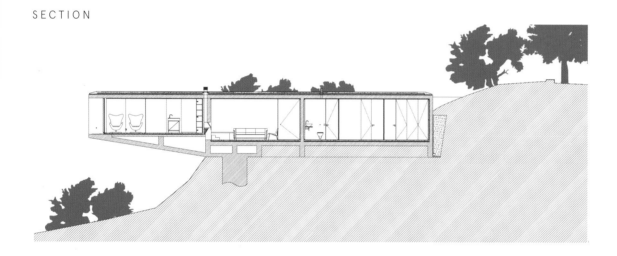

FIRST FLOOR

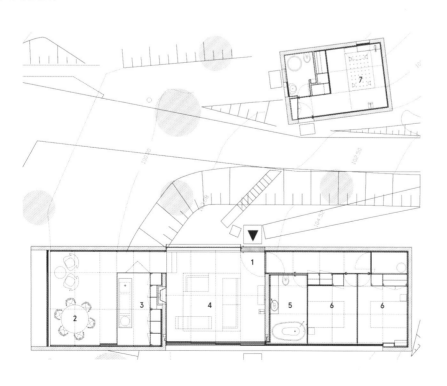

SITE PLAN

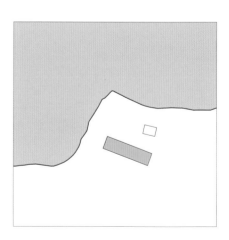

"From the house, the water should always be in the line of sight. But when you pass the house from the river, it should disappear into the vegetation."

CORREIA / RAGAZZI ——

The staircase from the path to the house and the ruin. Top: the light-colored birch interior contrasts with the coarse exposed concrete of floors and facade.

HOUSE IN BRIONE

Architects **MARKUS WESPI** and **JÉRÔME DE MEURON** outwitted the chaos and sprawl of Tessin. Their small villa overlooks the lake.

The quietness in front of the lake: natural stone blocks keep the hubbub of the popular area away and focus the senses on what is important—nature.
To the right, the interior patio and the large living room and kitchen.

FIRST FLOOR

TOP FLOOR

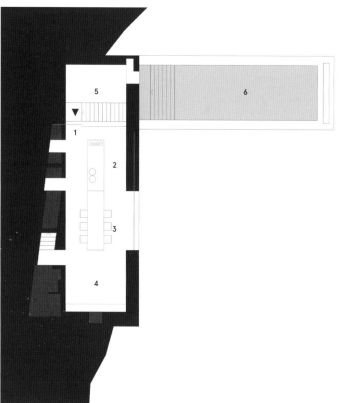

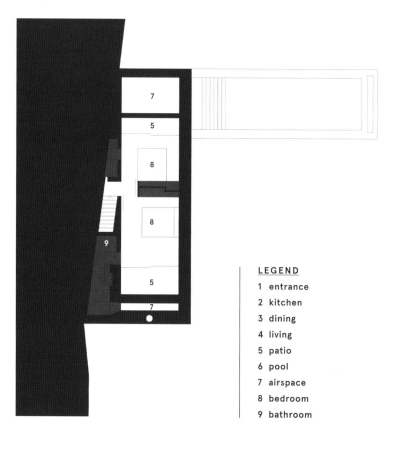

<u>LEGEND</u>

1 entrance
2 kitchen
3 dining
4 living
5 patio
6 pool
7 airspace
8 bedroom
9 bathroom

PROJECT DATA

Wespi de Meuron
Markus Wespi,
Jérôme de Meuron
Architekten BSA AG

lot area:
533 m² (5,737 ft²)
living area:
95 m² (1,023 ft²)

SECTION

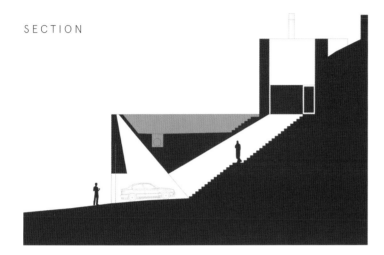

How should we build in a densely populated neighborhood? Tessin architects Markus Wespi and Jérôme de Meuron thought for a long time about their design on the hillside over Lake Maggiore and then rejected the attributes of a classical villa. Rather, they devised two blocks connected to each other via an internal staircase, covered in massive stone, that resembles sections of a city wall.

The area of Brione sopra Minusio has been crowded for quite some time. The dense residential neighborhood over Locarno with a view of the city, the lake, and the Alps was not meant to get another conventional building, the owner and the architects decided. Rather, it should be an oasis of quiet and self-discovery. As the architects described their concept, "Two basic-shaped stone cubes offset from each other protrude from the mountain, fragmentary, belonging more to the landscape than the building, more of a wall than a house, resisting a temporal attribution."

It took eighteen months to build this outstanding house of only 95 square meters (1,023 square feet). Interior rooms with stone floors and walls were created by excavation. Two similar gates provide access to this kingdom of minimalism—and a view. Interior patios let in light. The valley-side cube serves as a garage and its roof as a pool: the water seems to blend with the Lake Maggiore below. "The theme of water—both near and far —was really essential for this design," says Jérôme de Meuron.

In the garage cube, the basin's exposed concrete trough provides a strong contrast to the omnipresent natural stone, while light reflections through the narrow opening between the roof pool and wall enter the castle-like room. A wide, ceiling-high window faces south toward a small garden and the lake, in contrast to the closed cubes

WATERMILL —— 2004

WRITING WITH LIGHT HOUSE

New York architect <u>STEVEN HOLL</u> based the design of a Long Island summer home on the surrounding dune fences. The open wood frame invites daylight to play like a restless creative artist throughout the day.

SECTION

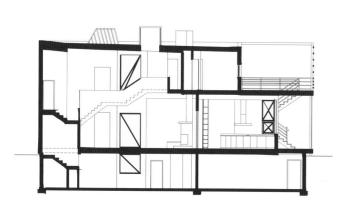

SITE PLAN

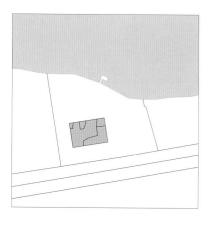

FIRST FLOOR $\oplus$

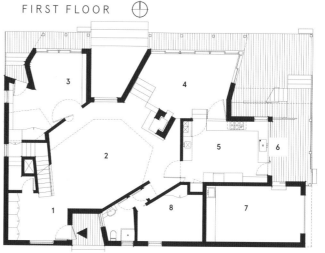

TOP FLOOR

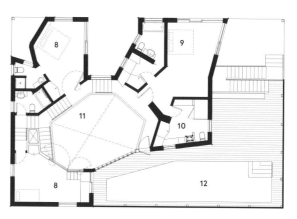

PROJECT DATA

Steven Holl Architects

covered area:
1,676 m² (18,040 ft²)
living area:
511 m² (5,500 ft²)
number of residents: 2

LEGEND

1 access
2 living
3 library
4 dining
5 kitchen
6 terrace
7 garage
8 guests
9 bedroom
10 bathroom
11 open to below
12 pool

Indian summer on Long Island: between creek,
pond, and bay, life is light and free.
The rooftop pool provides a view of the Atlantic (left page).

House of light: below is the octogonal living
room with a gallery. The local dune fences were the
main inspiration for the wood framing (right).

The narrow wooden posts of Hamptons dune fences inspired the lightweight balloon framing on this seaside vacation home for two. Architect Steven Holl was also influenced by the painter Jackson Pollock's 1949 oil painting *There Were Seven in Eight*. Pollock was a pioneer of abstract American Expressionism, and his former studio is in East Hampton close to the Writing with Light House on the Atlantic Ocean.

Opening toward the north, the elegantly frayed building ensemble is held together visually by the horizontal wood framing, which includes an exterior staircase.

Beams replace solid walls; the streaks of light permeating the interior connect it dynamically with the sun's daily cycle, and whitewashed interior walls amplify that effect.

Several guest rooms are distributed around the two-level octagonal living room in the center. From the living room you reach the top floor with an atrium, and a pool sits over the garage.

Between traditional wood and masonry houses stands a luminous apparition. The white residence at Lake Drevviken is unique, not only for its color. CLAESSON KOIVISTO RUNE took advantage of the property's width to provide a view of the lake from nearly every room.

DREVVIKEN HOUSE

STOCKHOLM —— 2010

"The house has its own small bay," explains architect Mårten Claesson. "Here the topography has a small depression. Hence the roof and ground lines are gently curved. They follow the terrain." All rooms except one face the lake.

LAYOUT

The lake property lies between two rocks on unstable ground. It had to be filled with stones to a depth of 12 meters (39 feet) and rests on a concrete slab. Note the varying heights of the rooms and the steps that equalize them.

SECTION

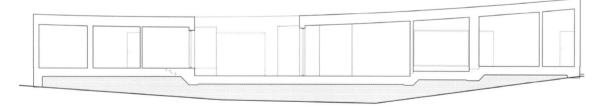

PROJECT DATA

Claesson Koivisto Rune Arkitektkontor AB

living area:
280 m² (3,014 ft²)

FIRST FLOOR

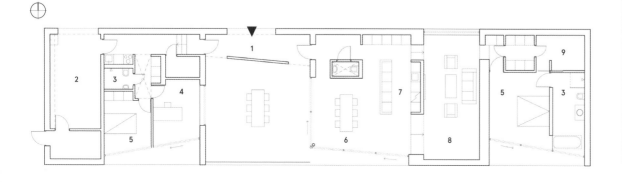

LEGEND

1 entrance
2 garage
3 bathroom
4 office
5 bedroom
6 dining
7 kitchen
8 living
9 dressing area

"You will be surprised by how small this home really is," says the owner, Tor Nielsen, at the door. It is ten minutes by car to the south of Stockholm, and 280 square meters (3,014 square feet) are quite a lot for guests from densely populated Central Europe. His point becomes quickly obvious, however: the architecture renounces the lounging area common in this type of home. Instead, one arrives inside a small wood-clad vestibule. Two meters (six and a half feet) away is a glass door, and from there the view expands over the formidable atrium terrace that constitutes a wonderful open-air living room and out to the glittering surface of Lake Drevviken .

The most unusual feature of this contemporary lake villa is the 35-meter-long (114-foot-long) street facade that resembles an unfurled sail. Stockholm architects Mårten Claesson, Eero Koivisto, and Ola Rune developed the design from the dominant vantage point of a nearby street crossing. Their intent was to align almost all of the rooms in a row, each with access to the lake on the narrow shoreline. Claesson Koivisto Rune converted the irregularity of the terrain into an asset by organizing the rooms with small landings on three levels. The room heights, varying between 3 and 4 meters (9 and 13 feet), are absorbed by an elegant upward line. The minimalism of the bright white facade is emphasized by three darker, asymmetrically arranged elements: garage gate, entrance door, and a window with a metal frame.

The firm is known for creating optical illusions with trapezoid and parallelogram shapes. MoMA design curator Paula Antonelli has likened these cuts and folds to origami, the art of folding paper.[1] The Swedish architects have used this wealth of motifs to create varied shapes without resorting to curved lines. Examples include a house on Gotland[2] and the Örsta Gallery in Kumla from 2010. There, too, they created angular window walls.

The bedroom features teak floors.
Comfort and coziness were important to the client.
The street facade is 35 meters (114 feet) long.

The office—with a view of the lake, of course!
Claesson Koivisto Rune also designed the small desk lamp.

"I wanted a house that did not exist here—yet!"

OWNER TOR NIELSEN ——

The house's folds and gentle rise are striking, whether you are driving past or directly toward it. In addition, the front is reminiscent of Alvar Aalto's gently rounded studio in Munkkiniemi close to Helsinki.[3] The interiors also reflect Aalto's concept of large, neatly arranged, well-shaped rooms. So it's not surprising that they are furnished with pieces by Aalto, along with utensils by Claesson Koivisto Rune.

Nielsen learned to know the architects when he lived for a few years in the hip Stockholm area of Södermalm, where their office is located. When the existing derelict building was demolished, the soil beneath it turned out to be unstable. The builders reached rock at a depth of 11 to 12 meters (36 to 39 feet) and filled the foundation with stones.

His new house catches the eye as an abstract sculpture. The rooms are arranged in a row on both sides of the atrium, with an apartment for his grown daughter to the right. Each room is accessed from the terrace or a narrow corridor. The living room features the only solid wall; it is oriented toward the lake and a large window faces the street. This gesture was important to the client, as he grew up only a few houses from here and knows many neighbors.

From the water side, a white concrete beam straddles the terrace atrium as an open frame. It adds rectilinear cohesiveness to the lake facade and also staggers the views. One would hardly notice the single-level house with its own bay next to the older two-level villas with their Swedish roofs "pulled over the ears" if it were not so white. Nielsen respected his architects' favorite color. However, he wished for a red room—hence the kitchen's reddish teak floor.

[1] See *Claesson Koivisto Rune, Architecture, Basel – Boston – Berlin* 2007. Preface by Paula Antonelli. The architects built the House of Culture in Kyoto for the Japanese company Sfera and designed a cotton armchair "cut and folded like origami."

[2] Ibid., Werner House, page 86.

[3] Alvar Aalto's studio, built in 1955, creates a concave facade curve for the exhibition hall for models and drawings that sweeps upward and envelops the amphitheater in the patio.

The dining room features modernist white tiles. The armchairs and dining table are Hans Wegner classics.

SOUTH PACIFIC —— 2012

CASA BOUHON IN MA- TANZAS

WMR ARQUITECTOS built a series of simple, elegant wood houses on a surfing beach in Chile. This is the most recent one.

SECTION

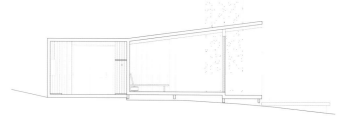

FIRST FLOOR

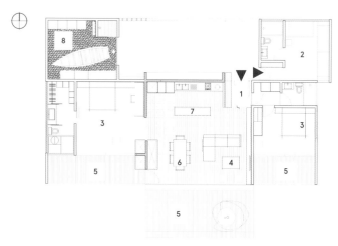

SITE PLAN

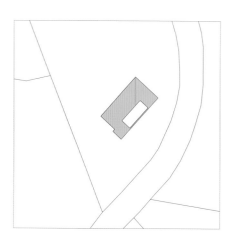

PROJECT DATA
WMR Arquitectos
Felipe Wedeless,
Jorge Manieu,
Macarena Rabat

LEGEND
1 entrance
2 guests
3 bedroom
4 living
5 terrace
6 dining
7 kitchen
8 boat storage

Sports and fun: evenings after surfing, the central exposed concrete fireplace warms the sportsmen. It can be controlled from inside and outside.
To the left, the house facade facing the Pacific. Below, in the foreground, the guest suite.

Matanzas is some two to three hours by car from Santiago de Chile. WMR Arquitectos—Felipe Wedeles, Jorge Manieu, und Macarena Rabat—have built several large and small buildings on one of the beaches—casas and cabañas, and even a hotel. Now there are three new vacation homes: Casa 3 Hermanos, Casa Puccio, and the latest one, Casa Bouhon.

Like many of the homes here, this weekend residence was built for surfers. It sits high up on the hillside and offers a stupendous view. One could call it a box on stilts because it is supported by a raised wood platform. Two smaller units hide behind the first one, and the entrance is between them. The front section has a monopitch roof. Ceiling-high windows face the ocean along the entire front. Incised terraces on wood planks are located outside the lateral rooms, which receive additional light via horizontal, slit-shaped windows that separate and structure the design. Additionally, the protrusions provide a protective roof to sit under outdoors during windy or rainy weather. The single-level house is outfitted simply and practically with wood floors and walls. At its center is a large exposed concrete fireplace that can be used from both inside and outside. A large sliding door closes off the living room and kitchen from the bedroom. From the land side, a storage space for boards and boats is attached to the residence. An additional bedroom on the rear level can be accessed separately and used as a guest apartment.

Black clinker masonry provides an earthy counterpoint on a lake house designed by **BEDAUX DE BROUWER ARCHITECTES** in the Dutch province of Zeeland.

VILLA IN KAMPER-LAND

VEERSE MEER —— 2009

FIRST FLOOR

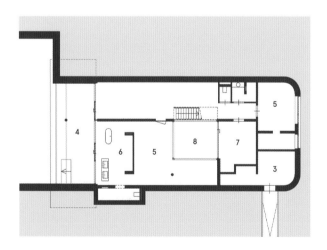

SECTION

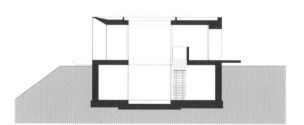

TOP FLOOR

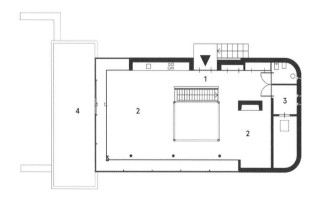

PROJECT DATA

Bedaux de Brouwer
Architecten BV BNA
Jacques de Brouwer

lot size:
994 m² (10,700 ft²)
living area:
360 m² (3,875 ft²)

LEGEND

1 entrance
2 living
3 storage
4 terrace
5 bedroom
6 bathroom
7 office
8 atrium

Chiaroscuro, Dutch version: a glass atrium provides plenty of light, even down to the bedrooms.
Toward the front and the water the house is completely open. The other sides takes an
almost defensive stance via a matte black clinker facade (left).

"We practically live inside this great view!"

THE OWNERS ——

This house lies along the slightly rising shore of the Veerse Meer inland lake, which was separated from the North Sea in 1961. It offers a panoramic view of the lake and boat jetty from a generous balcony outside the glassy, 106-square-meter (1,141-square-foot) dining and living area.

Ceramic clinker wraps all four sides of the two-story, flat-roofed building, lending a calm and uniform facade. The masonry's dark joints amplify the monolithic effect, says Jacques de Brouwer. The building's edges are rounded, and the northeastern side facing the street features a narrow vertical gap that adds interest to the closed facade. Here the villa appears protective and forbidding; the window slits look like the barbicans of a castle. The slightly recessed entrance with wide concrete steps and the black door oriented northwest also have a reserved appearance.

The interiors, outfitted by the interior design firm Annega & Partners, are light and airy. A 7-meter (23-foot)-high glass atrium at the house's center illuminates the lower-level bedrooms while providing the main living level with uninterrupted views of the lake.

The two corners of the building flowing around the edge toward the street elegantly mediate between the transparency of the waterfront and the expressive massiveness of the black bricks. "We chose a double glass facade and hard, dark stone to provide good protection against inclement weather and the wear and tear of time," says Jacques de Brouwer, adding: "We are proud of the fact that we managed this project with a minimum of materials while creating an expressive residence for the owners." The owners' favorite place in the house is at the heart of the glass cockpit with a view of the Veerse Meer, the dramatic Dutch skies, and the silhouette of the Veere village on the opposite shore.

CONTEM-PORARY RUSTICO

SARDINIA
—— 2004

ANTONIO CITTERIO and **PATRICIA VIEL** replaced an overly large farmhouse from the 1960s on the southern part of the island. The new structure is lined with dry stone walls and fits naturally between the water and hilly landscape.

"What a stroke of luck! The client was most interested in building culture, the light, and the beauty of the surroundings. For the first two months we talked only about Sardinian architecture."

ANTONIO CITTERIO ——

Deep windowsills provide protection from the harsh sun.
Downstairs is the owner's private area with the south-facing terrace and a view of the citrus garden. Guest rooms are upstairs.

A country home without boundaries: only light, location, structure, and nature influenced
Antonio Citterio's design consisting of dry stone walls and white sand cement walls.

You can't build this close to the coast anymore, except when an existing building is replaced. And when it came time to restructure the building and landscape in Villasimius, not far from Cagliari, it was clear that the new home would be inconspicuous. The Milan architect Antonio Citterio is well-known for his aversion to the ostentatious, soft pink and peach-colored homes along the Northern Sardinian coast of Costa Smeralda.

"I wanted to surround the house with gardens and patios. And with dry stone walls to keep the wind at bay,"[1] Citterio explains. The architect and his client chose the color white for the main top section of the building and gave it a deliberately imperfect finish of irregular, rough lime plaster rounded along the edges. The first floor, built with granite and several stone walls, interweaves the building and landscape of vineyards and citrus and olive orchards—part of an agricultural business comprising many acres.

The house lies 6 meters (20 feet) above the beach. An additional stone wall provides a boundary to the water. The various walls and foundations reduce the building's perceived massiveness—it is the only building in the area, and it is remarkable that 450 square meters (4,844 square feet) of living area plus 300 square meters (3,229 square feet) of terraces can be hidden this well.

The architects maintained the original building's footprint while entirely changing its exterior. "New gangways resulted in a better relationship between interior and exterior,"[2] Citterio explains. Walls 45 centimeters (1.5 feet) thick and deep openings help to shade the interiors and keep them cool, like the traditional farmhouse did. "We spent a lot of time at the computer simulating the position of the sun at different times of day," Citterio says. "Light shining into the rooms was to be entirely avoided."[3] As the windowsills broaden toward the exterior, the view of the sea is also wider.

Citterio's big idea was also his most difficult task: to reinterpret the relationship between landscape and building. The house sits on the lowest part of the property. The lot rises over the hillside and expands southward to the cultivated landscape. As Alba Cappellieri once pointed out, the house is not the center "but only part of a mosaic."[4] Its relative lightness is mainly due to the expertly created "floating" structure that forms a moderate white contrast to the hillside and natural stone walls.

Critterio was inspired by Mies van der Rohe's use of rustic elements as a protective counterpoint to modernism's materials. In the 1920s he outfitted white, flat-roofed houses with stone foundations. Critterio chose gray basalt flooring slabs, teak frames for the windows and sliding doors, and noble, ascetic furnishings.

[1] See *Architectural Digest* 4 / 2006, page 54, Antonio Citterio
   in an interview with the author, January 2006, Milan.
[2 + 3] Ibid.
[4] See page 187 in: Alba Cappellieri, "Antonio Citterio" –
   Architecture and Design, Milan, 2007.

The citrus garden sits inside a
wind-protected patio.

SECTION

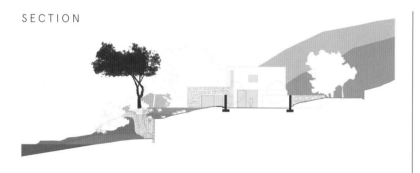

FIRST FLOOR

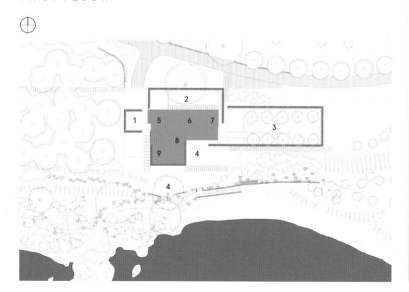

PROJECT DATA

Antonio Citterio,
Patricia Viel and Partners

lot size:
35 ha (87 acres)
living area:
450 m² (4,849 ft²) plus
300 m² (3,229 ft²) of
terraces, 425 m² (4,575 ft²)
of citrus grove and 200
m² (2,153 ft²) of patios

LEGEND
1 outdoor kitchen
2 patio
3 citrus garden
4 terrace
5 kitchen
6 bathroom
7 bedroom
8 living
9 dining

Tutto Citterio: it helps when the architect is also a famous interior designer.
His armchairs and daybeds furnish the living room.

The owners wake up to the sky and sea.

Long live the escarpment!
<u>BEMBÉ DELLINGER
ARCHITEKTEN</u> aimed high to
provide as much forest, light, and
river as possible for its client.

TWIN HOUSE

GRAFRATH —— 2007

AT THE AMPER

SECTION

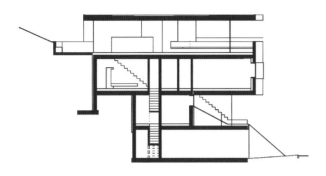

FIRST FLOOR

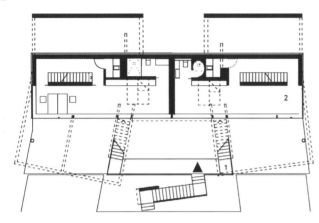

SECOND FLOOR

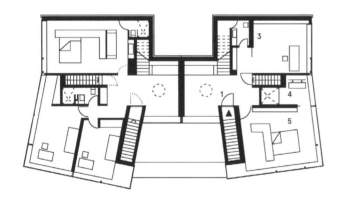

THIRD FLOOR

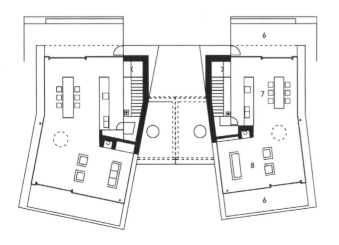

SITE PLAN

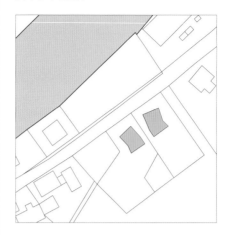

PROJECT DATA

Bembé Dellinger
Architekten und
Stadtplaner GmbH

lot size:
1,591 m² (17,130 ft²)
living/terrace area:
411/92 m² (4,424/990 ft²)
residents: 2–3

LEGEND

1 entrance
2 guests
3 office
4 bathroom
5 bedroom
6 terrace
7 kitchen/dining
8 living

Sebastian Dellinger shakes his head as he remembers one of the most demanding building sites of his life. "This place had exasperated several architects before us!" However, Dellinger and his partner Felix Bembé took on the challenge. The two young architects and their team have built many houses in a deliberately international style, particularly in Upper Bavaria. And once again they had the right idea in Grafrath, close to Lake Ammer.

The lot was challenging: a steep hillside between the river Amper to the northwest and an old-growth beech forest to the southeast. A steep hill above the small service road had to be painstakingly removed to adequately anchor the steel and concrete structure into the narrow area, and it took the excavator six weeks to move the accumulated gravel back into the pit.

"You are sitting high up next to the treetops. Fish are down in the river and the deer are standing on the terrace."

SEBASTIAN DELLINGER ——

The plane overhanging the top floor is wood frame construction reinforced with steel girders (opposite page). Above, the open living room has oiled wood flooring. Its terrace sits about 20 meters (66 feet) above the river. The opposite side of the living room opens to a ground level terrace that meets the hillside.

The four-level building was divided in two to reduce its scale and house twin units. "We wanted to reach as high as possible—toward the sun, always with a view of the water and the riverside forest," Dellinger says,

"The owners step up from the garage level and the bedroom level, toward the light and the living room," he says. There is ample light, a direct view connection to the river, and the impression that you are more or less standing in the middle of the forest. Skylights with silver funnels under the roof amplify the collected sunlight. Nature is always in the foreground.

However, the structure does not defer to nature but exudes its own confidence. Board-formed concrete wraps both buildings, which are offset by a few degrees and face different directions. One of the wings has just under 200 square meters (2,152 square feet) of living space, the other slightly more. Each house has a small lawn at the water, and a pier.

The owners access their home from the double garages, while visitors and pedestrians use the exterior staircases. Each narrow, exposed concrete interior staircase leads past the vehicles, which are visible through the windows, to a second floor that is cool even on hot days. This floor contains an office or guest room. The third floor houses three bedrooms, one with a panoramic window. The luminous, open living area on the fourth floor includes two terraces: one is level with the hillside, the other is high above the street and river. And a third terrace takes in views from the roof. Le Corbusier's work is recalled in the thin pilotis, long windows, and a white sun-shade that pushes over the terraces like a brise soleil.

VILLA

A large house for guests and the arts: <u>ANTONELLA RUPP</u> went through the drama of building for herself high above Lake Constance, and succeeded.

LAKE CONSTANCE —— 2008

RUPP

Large interlocking cubes:
Antonella Rupp has been influenced by Álvaro Siza and the
rationalists of modernism. Shown here are the benches on
the pool level; on top is the living area.

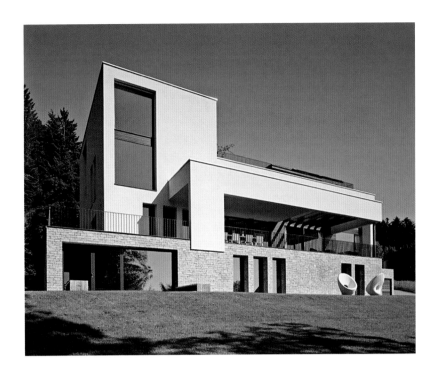

"Nothing I do is filigree — and I am proud of it."

ANTONELLA RUPP ——

The proud view of the Villa Rupp in Eichenberg.
Guests stay in the tower.

Architect Antonella Rupp from Lake Como always knew one thing: that her dream house on the lake would one day be a reality. A few years ago she discovered a lot overlooking Lake Constance surrounded by forests and meadows. It seemed like the perfect site for a spacious house that could accommodate large gatherings. She also envisioned terraces where she could spend time when the weather was pleasant.

Situated on a hillside between Lindau and Bregenz, the Villa Rupp has a Pietra di Luserna granite base, interlocking cubes, and an understated tower that provides a view as far as Lindau Island. The compositional elements seamlessly assimilate the spatial interpenetrations of classic architectural modernism. Giò Ponti, Carlo Scarpa, and rationalists such as Giuseppe Terragni and Adalberto Libera are Rupp's paragons. The contemporary floor plan takes into account that people today demand generous bedrooms and bathrooms and that the living area can be open on all sides. The house is large and transparent, yet it does not present itself as a stage to the neighbors, and the generous pool by British artist Gary Hume fits the house's spirit and style. Rupp made her first sketch as early as 2003 in her sister's apartment in Rome, basing it on an initial instinct for a longish building with a protruding tower. "Later I tried out curves and ramps, which were not necessary, really," she says. "Sometimes I felt like a student!"

At one point her husband, Josef Rupp, threatened, "If you don't start building, I will order a prefabricated home that you will have to move into." Rupp smiles: "Those times of decision-making were the most difficult of my life!" When she returned to her first sketches, everything came together. "The sketch contained all of the essential elements. The first idea—clear lines and proportions—had been the best one," she says.

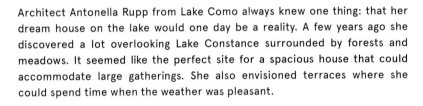

The ipe wood was imported from Brazil; the pathway becomes part of the entrance facade.

SECTION

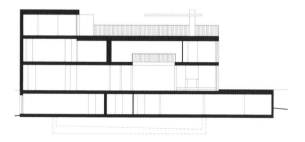

FIRST FLOOR

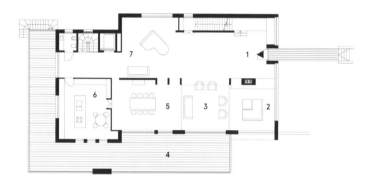

A view as if painted by Caspar David Friedrich. It eliminates boundaries to the fireplace room. Below, the pool level. The artist GaryHume designed it with mosaic tiles from Bisazza.

SECOND FLOOR

THIRD FLOOR

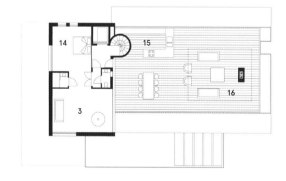

PROJECT DATA
Architekturbüro
Antonella Rupp GmbH

lot size:
2,070 m² (22,280 ft²)
living/terrace area:
1,170/986 m²
(12,594/10,610 ft²)
residents: 3

LEGEND
1 entrance
2 fireplace
3 living
4 terrace
5 dining
6 kitchen
7 music room
8 library
9 office
10 playroom
11 airspace
12 dressing area
13 bathroom
14 bedroom
15 summer kitchen
16 lounge/fireplace

The large living hall comprising two floors often
functions as a salon. The smokers meet at the chimney.
Custom-made sofa by Romeo Sozzi.
The architect designed much of the furniture. Her
husband, Josef Rupp, collects Chinese horses.

In the skies above Lake Constance:
On clear days you can see from the Villa
Rupp to the island of Lindau.

"During summer we live on our terraces most of the time," says architect and owner Antonella Rupp.

Rupp's 1,170-square-meter (12,594-square-foot) residence is based more on contemporary designers such as Rafael Moneo and Álvaro Siza than on the Vorarlberg building tradition. Its four stories—pool level, double-height living level, and bedroom with roof terrace—can be accessed by elevator. Stone for the fireplace and bathrooms came from the quarries of her friend Deborah Morceletto, whose company headquarters are near Vicenza, and with whom Carlo Scarpa worked. Antonella Rupp studied in Milan with industrial designer Achille Castiglione, and many of the sofas, tables, and armchairs are custom made.

Outside, a flaming Brazilian ipe pathway runs across the lawn before rising up to the roof, a vertical band on the cream-colored facade. Some of the interior flooring is oiled with black pigment. These exotic and elegant details are typical: the Rupps like to spice up their lives with items they find on vacation. "When we come back from Brazil we always bring two containers full of stuff," she says.

The house is designed for art. Paintings by Czech cubists and photos from Brazil coexist with Chinese terracotta horses from various epochs of the Han dynasty, Tang empire, and western and eastern Zhou period.

Much of the Rupp villa belongs to the guests. "We have lots of invited guests —summer parties, small private house concerts, and relaxed jazz evenings," she says. Such events reveal the material connection between inside and outside: seating facilities, woods, and bronze materials repeat. Rupp is a consumate host who sometimes offers the best accommodations to friends or artists who are preparing for the Bregenz festival: the top deck with summer kitchen and two suites that can be combined or separated with rolling walls. From up there, king-size windows provide spectacular views across the lake.

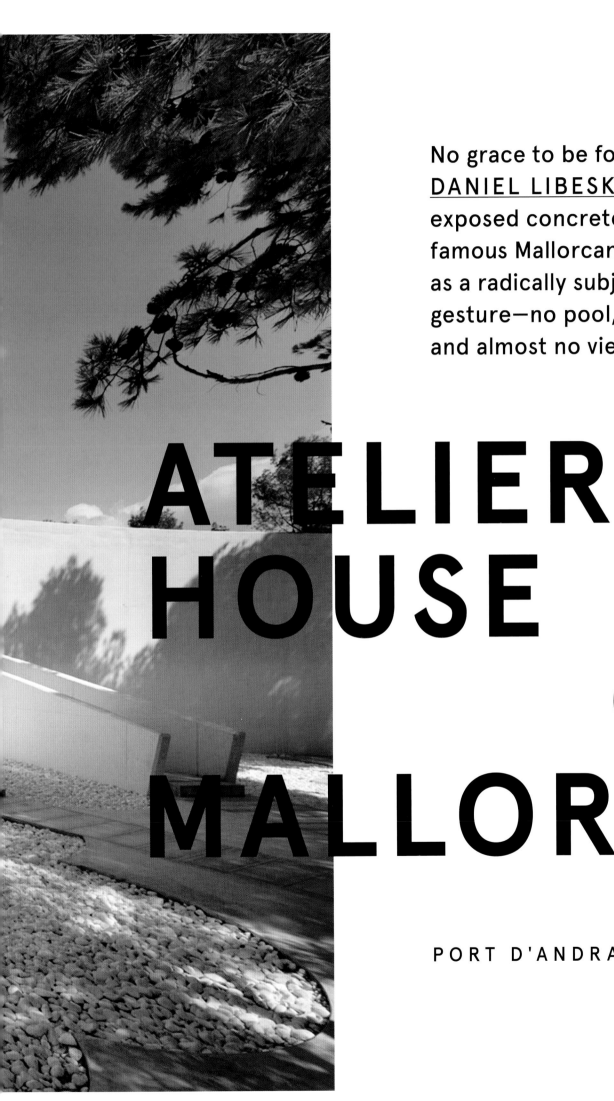

No grace to be found anywhere: <u>DANIEL LIBESKIND</u> built an exposed concrete villa at a famous Mallorcan vacation spot as a radically subjective gesture—no pool, no deck chair, and almost no views.

ATELIER HOUSE ON MALLORCA

PORT D'ANDRATX —— 2003

"This is not an anti-villa but an alternative to conventional private residences."

DANIEL LIBESKIND ——

Less is more.
Only a stepped pathway leads to the
light and the water view.

While designing his first large institutional projects, Daniel Libeskind spent several years working on a private residence on Mallorca for an American artist who has been living on the island since the 1970s. The sculptor and painter commissioned a residence that would also be a studio, storage place, and showroom. Viewed from the opposite coast, an unidentifiable white block lurks on the hillside. From the port city of Port d'Antratx, you only have to follow the coast road. Set among celebrity estates, a huge, oblique white poured concrete wall suddenly appears, curving back and forth. It is closed off toward the street, but also toward the bay and the sun: no windows, no balconies—only a small lookout with a balustrade at the end of a long staircase that divides the building.

Viewed from the side, Libeskind's wall front looks like a swaying ship. The wall has no windows, only an exit, a band of light, and some Libeskind-style cuts and notches. It certainly is different from the surrounding neo-rustic estates. Nearly every surface—floors, walls, ceilings, and staircases—consist of exposed concrete.

It took five years to conclude this small opus. During construction the architect moved his company from Berlin to New York after winning the bid for Ground Zero. Libeskind has remained faithful to his program of complex yet open, low-budget projects with many cuts and voids. Nevertheless, he has shed some skin. Instead of the extroverted zigzag of his three museums in Berlin, Osnabrück, and Liverpool that were created during the same period, this residence consists of soft segments of non-concentric circles, as he describes it.[1] The circles are based on the "mnemonic wheels" of the medieval mystic Ramon Llull born in 1232 in Palma de Mallorca. One could describe it as regionalism à la Libeskind. The

architect, who loves philosophical correlations between the past and present, was fascinated by the allegory of the "thought islands" that disappear and reappear. And the fact that many of the circles have centers. "You never arrive," says its creator.[2] This residence has no center and no objective: "The harmony lies in the contrasts," he says. The effect is that of being on a permanent "*promenade architecturale.*" One constantly has to think about how to get from one studio to the other, visible through slits in the walls or glass facades. The resident doesn't mind; she wanted it that way.

Zen meets industrial style: the patio of the house on Mallorca is designed like an Isamu Noguchi playground. The industrial staircase in the background divides the building and leads from the patio to the only view of the ocean. At the top is a sketch where Libeskind pre-planned the view and the staircase as early as 1998.

The landscape is Mediterranean, the house is cool and hermetic. Shown here is the great location as seen from the opposite coast.

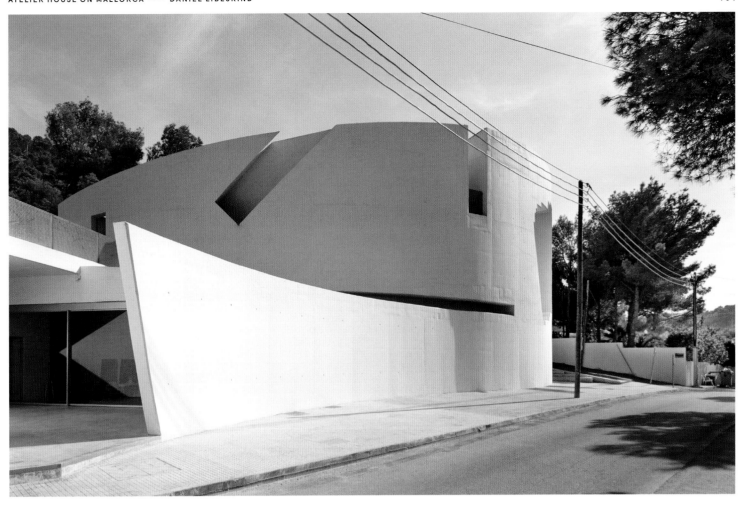

Cuts à la Libeskind: the cuts and openings provide structure to the exposed concrete. The villa faces away from the ocean and toward the owner's art (below).

The surprising interior patio, with its white stone basins, is reminiscent of the playgrounds and Zen gardens of the artist and landscape designer Isamu Noguchi. Precise wall incisions allow for light or sections of sky to enter. However, the chain-link fences, industrial grids, and many oblique and slanted planes keep this from being a contemplative environment. "After all, what do you really need? A table, a bed, a few musical instruments,"[3] Libeskind says.

The artist designed her home in close collaboration with the architect. As she says, she is able to work and breathe freely. Meanwhile, guests in this home know that they have to forgo glamour, large pieces of furniture, expensive accessories—and a choice view of the ocean.

[1] See "Mnemonic Cartwheels," in: catalog for a Libeskind exhibition at Aedes West, Berlin, 2000, page 7.

[2] See Alexander Hosch, "Die Villa zur Macht" ("The Villa to Power"), in: *Süddeutsche Zeitung*, Feuilleton , page 15, 2003.

[3] From a telephone interview between Daniel Libeskind and the author in 2005, published in the *SZ Magazine* No. 13, 1.4. 2005, page 18.

STOCKHOLM
SCHÄRENGARTEN —— 2009

HUSET PÅ KLIPPAN

Silvery spruce and huge glass windows characterize the look of the residence that <u>PETRA GIPP</u> and <u>KATARINA LUNDEBERG</u> designed on a cliff on a Stockholm archipelago.

"We put much emphasis on elegantly aging materials," says Petra Gipp. Opposite below, the view from the entrance into the open living room and nature. This is the architect's favorite place: "The boundaries between inside and outside dissolve."

SECTION

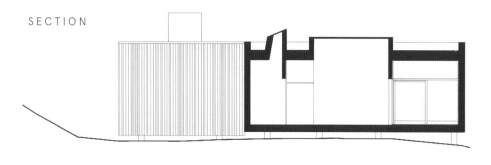

FIRST FLOOR

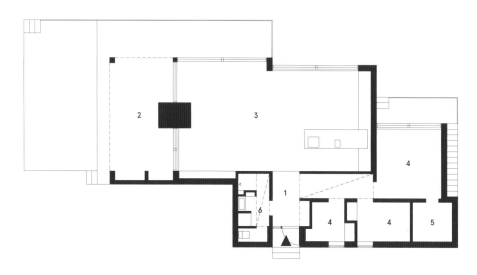

PROJECT DATA

Petra Gipp Arkitektur AB
and Katarina Lundeberg
In Praise of Shadows AB

lot size:
2,600 m² (27,990 ft²)
living area:
150 m² (1,615 ft²)
residents: 2

LEGEND

1 access
2 lounge
3 living/kitchen
4 bedroom
5 dressing room
6 bathroom

SITE PLAN

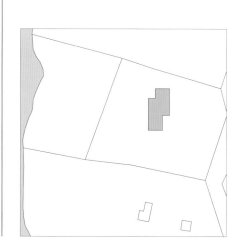

The white siding is covered with ferrous sulfate.
Spruce was used for the floors and the kitchen block
inside the open living room.

The owner of this home wanted to focus on nature and have as much privacy as possible. This resulted in a transparent design that turns away from the neighboring vacation homes dating to around 1900 and faces the water. The home sits on the tip of a cape, 28 meters (92 feet) high on a cliff, and the view is astounding. In some rooms you can see the entire bay.

There are two volumes, which are separated internally. One is closed off and contains the private quarters; there are several bedrooms with separate entrances. The larger bedroom accesses an adjacent terrace and a bathroom that is open at the top. The other volume with the huge windows facing the Baltic Sea bay is dedicated to the more public aspects. The kitchen is integrated into the large living room. The two units are separated by a "light fountain" that slices through the house. This is created by daylight entering through a large "lantern" on top of the tower.

The home on the cliff makes for an elegant and contemporary "bella figura." The volumes look as if they could be separated and pushed back together again.

Architect Petra Gipp considers this closed internal plane to be the strongest element of her design. "The client wanted the terraces, the house, and the cliff to be a cohesive unit," she says. "In order to achieve a formal unit, I integrated the generous terraces into the structure of the building. At the same time they provide a bond with the ground."

Staircases are worked out from the cubic geometry that connects the ground and bedroom terrace and the bedroom terrace with the roof. The foundation floats over the property, leaving the landscape untouched.

Materials and detailing underscore the restrained design, which is reduced to only a few colors and features: the boarding panels are of varying size and partially coated white. The edges are beveled. Floors and some of the walls consist of spruce boards. Poured concrete and galvanized sheet metal was selected for its natural look as it ages.

CAP FERRET —— 1998

MAISON À L'ATLANTIQUE

Trees that grow through the roof:
toward the end of the last millennium, this home by
LACATON and VASSAL ARCHITECTES on the
French Atlantic coast was the trailblazer for a new
relationship between humans, architecture, and nature.

At a time when houses could hardly be larger or more spectacular, this project on the Bay of Arcachon close to Bordeaux outdoes itself. Parisian architects Anne Lacaton and Jean-Philippe Vassal planned a home in a protective landscape on a southeast-facing lot that had been lying undeveloped for a long time. The goal was to spare both the surroundings and the client's budget, without sacrificing the quality of the design. To avoid cutting down any of the forty-six pine trees on the land or disturbing the flat dunes vegetation mimosa and arbutus, the home was raised on twelve galvanized steel columns. They reach some eight to ten meters (twenty-six to thirty-three feet) into the sandy ground. This helped to preserve the view of the bay from the water.

A seismic frame acts as a visible structural support. The terrain, which falls steeply and abruptly toward the ocean, was not only preserved with its existing vegetation, but some of the trees towering over the house actually perforate the building. They function as a kind of spatial divider and add appeal to a vacation home that blends almost imperceptibly into the landscape. Where the trees perforate the house they are provided with special support structures that accommodate their swaying and bending with the wind. The result is akin to a treehouse half the height of the treetops.

The grade difference between the living level and ground level was solved with a steel spiral staircase, and fifty more steps lead down to the beach. A traditional wood wall provides privacy near the narrow beach.

The facade is open or glazed facing the sea. The other three faces are more opaque and feature translucent polycarbonate panels. Obviously, Lacaton Vassal based its concept on the lightweight constructions of Jean Prouvé. By utilizing "poor materials" from industrial manufacturing such as chain-link fence, concrete screed, metal frames, polycarbonate, and corrugated sheet metal, they created a diaphanous and highly elegant shell.

There is enough headroom to walk upright under the house. The platform underside is clad in shiny silver aluminum that the architects call an "artificial sky." The undulating terrain and vertical columns and trees create surprising light and shadow effects and an otherworldly view of the Atlantic and its horizon.

PROJECT DATA
Lacaton Vassal Architects

living area:
180 m² (1,938 ft²) + 30 m² (323 ft²) terrace
residents: 2

Treehouse forever: supports in the concrete ceilings allow the pine trees to sway and bend.

Above, the view from the terrace to the terrain sloping down to the Bassin d'Arcachon.
Below left, the facade facing the sea, hidden inside the forest. The photo at the bottom right shows the translucent polycarbonate elements facing north.

SECTION

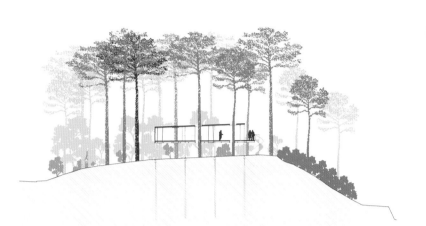

SITE PLAN

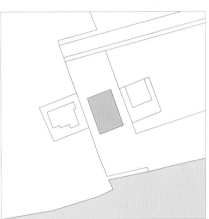

ARCHI-PELAGO

HUSARÖ ARCHIPELAGO —— 2006

HOUSE

An early project by
<u>THAM</u> and <u>VIDEGÅRD</u>:
a Stockholm family can
spend their weekends close
to nature between the
rocks, grass, bushes, trees,
and the Baltic Sea.

Living under a leaf canopy (left and top): the pine trees, pergola ribs, and black varnished wood panels of the Archipelago House allow for light to enter playfully. The shingle cladding protects and entertains the residents at the same time.

There are locations where the world seems to belong to you. This vacation home on the Husarö Island is one of them. In summer, the trip from Stockholm takes two hours by boat. And upon arrival at the pier, there is another fifteen-minute walk to the house, which faces the sea.

Little imagination is required to understand the effort it took to build this little spot of self-selected solitude. Building materials had to be brought by boat and were transported by every conceivable means, including carrying them on the shoulder. As a result, only lightweight materials such as wood could be used.

Materials also had to be sturdy because of the Nordic marine climate. This project was one of the first commissions for young architects Bolle Tham and Martin Videgård Hansson, and they incorporated bold elements such as black varnished wood panels. Its contemporary aesthetic is both practical and reminiscent of algorithm patterns.

The architects placed their parallelogram-shaped house on a platform between two rock formations. Three carefully selected specialists built the home in one and a half years almost entirely without additional help. They lived in a motor home next to the building site, even during winter.

The unobtrusive home faces south and west. The family enjoys a subtle play of light and views in 130 square meters (1,399 square feet). "It should feel like being under a leaf canopy,"[1] says Tham. The pine trees and dark pergola, combined with the light-colored decking, create a light-and-shadow play between interior and exterior.

Offsetting the different spaces—bedroom, living area, kitchen and children's room—along the rhythmic glass facade created an elegant solution to protection from the wind, and the sliding doors make life easier in this often stormy environment. Interiors are finished with white pine walls, oak floors, and light-colored furniture.

The living quarters' diagonally arranged glass boxes divert the wind. The sliding doors also help to deal with the often rough Nordic climate. At the top, the view of the living room at dusk; below is the row of cubes. Opposite, kitchen and dining table.

FIRST FLOOR

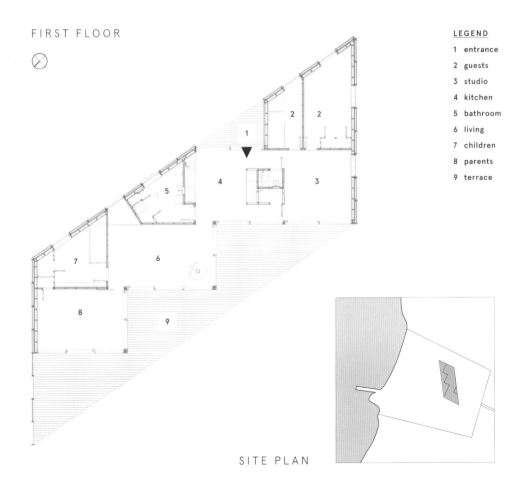

[1] see Bolle Tham in: *Architectural Digest*, 7/8 2007: "Nordisches Lichtspiel" ("Nordic light play"), page 48: "You should feel like you are under an illuminated leaf canopy."

SITE PLAN

LEGEND

1 entrance
2 guests
3 studio
4 kitchen
5 bathroom
6 living
7 children
8 parents
9 terrace

PROJECT DATA
Tham & Videgård Arkitekter
Bolle Tham & Martin Videgård

lot size:
3,250 m² (34,980 ft²
living area:
130 m² (1,399 f²)

HOUSE IN BEINWIL

DARLINGTON MEIER ARCHITEKTEN applied simplicity, beautiful materials, and a clever layout to this house not far from Zurich.

LAKE HALLWIL —— 2006

Swiss Study House: with a few clever tricks, the architects made the house float and "pulled" the lake closer. Now it is a presence in almost all of the rooms.

SECTION

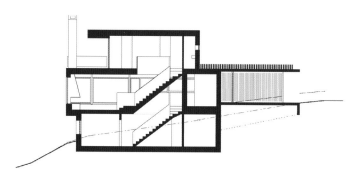

FIRST FLOOR

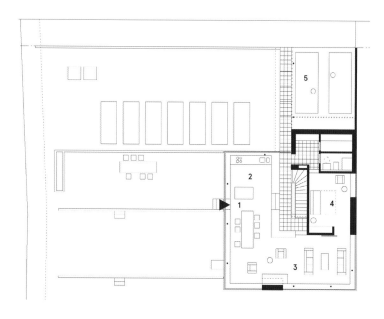

TOP FLOOR

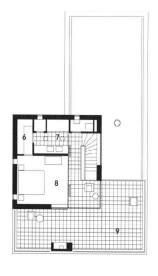

PROJECT DATA
Darlington Meier
Architekten
Mark Darlington,
Stephan Meier

lot size:
708 m² (7,621 ft²)
living area:
170/215 meters²
(1,830/2,314 ft²)
residents: 2
energy concept:
rainwater collection,
heat pump

LEGEND
1 entrance
2 kitchen/dining
3 living
4 library
5 carport
6 dressing area
7 bathroom
8 bedroom
9 terrace

Floors made of concrete or anhydrite (such as the living room below) are colored, sanded, and oiled.
The ceilings were left with a rough, exposed concrete finish.
A gem: the exterior fireplace (top).

"The lake panorama is a continuous companion in each room."

STEPHAN MEIER ——

The house at Lake Hallwil reminded the Swiss architectural press of the California Case Study houses from the 1940s and 1950s, and of Richard Neutra's work.[1] Architect Stephan Meier put the landscape front and center. "The panoramic view over the entire lake dominates the property and provides an ever-present backdrop," he says. "Our favorite place is the open-air spot framed by the exterior fireplace with an unobstructed view to the Alps."

A carport leads into this house like a pier. Behind the entrance area is the staircase, the hinge of the house, and suddenly you arrive at a "cockpit" with windows on all sides overlooking the lake. There you encounter the kitchen, dining and living areas, and library. This clever layout was economical and allowed for a sweeping view of the landscape from the first floor.

Materials were as carefully considered as the floor plan. The 170-square-meter (1,829-square-foot) interior features exposed concrete ceilings and plastered walls. Floors are made of concrete and anhydrite that has been dyed, sanded, and oiled. The edges of the building are rounded, and the circumferential, band-shaped aluminum window incorporates this motif. The monopitch roof includes plantings.

The exterior was plastered and whitewashed horizontally, then varnished with several layers of silver color. Those horizontal brush strokes contribute to the structure's refined appearance. "We purposely worked with subdued colors like white and light gray and consciously applied the varying levels of brilliance. They reflect the dominant light and transport it into the interior. For example, the balustrades feature enameled gray-green tiles," Meier says.

[1] See "Hochsitz über dem Hallwilersee" ("Perch over Lake Hallwil"), in: *Viso*, 03/2008, page 54; "Schlicht und einfach schön," ("Plain and simply beautiful"), in: *Sonntagszeitung*, 5.25.2008, page 83 and "In this Case," in: *Werk, Bauen + Wohnen* 1 / 2, 2009, page 48 2006, Milan.

WATER VILLA

AMSTERDAM —— 2010

DE OMVAL

Houseboats are for people who want to live in a trailer on the water, right? Wrong! **+31 ARCHITECTS** designed a luxury home that you can step aboard.

Cheerful living quarters instead of a dank cabin: sliding doors open the space to the light.
The split-level solution allowed for two floors.
Opposite: in a different kind of urban living, the owners live at eye-level with the river.
The Gehry armchair and customized built-in furniture proclaim that style is on board.

"This villa came to Amsterdam after a two-day journey on the water!"

JASPER SUASSO DE LIMA DE PRADO

AND JORRIT HOUWERT ——

Parts of the Netherlands lie below sea level, and living on the water has long been common. Today it is more popular than ever, particularly since global warming and rising sea levels have become part of the collective consciousness. Controlled flooding is an alternative to the country's elaborate construction of dams and dikes. The result is that new houses cannot be built in the ground; they have to swim. +31 Architects are specialists in this regard and have built a number of homes on the water. Their most sophisticated water house so far is one of their most recent: de Omval south of Amsterdam. There are two possibilities for building literally on the water, Jasper Suasso de Lima de Prado and Jorrit Houwert explain. The pontoon method involves building a solid floating platform that is lighter than water. The other variation is based on a boat: a hollow box made from steel and concrete that is open at the top. This type of house is more difficult to maneuver into shallow water than a pontoon house.

+31 architects typically uses the second method because the structure is more stable and the "space in the box" can be used for living quarters. The superstructure is supported by steel frames combined with steel ceiling profiles and wooden frames. However, much of the weight must be placed at the very bottom. To determine water displacement, the weight of the building above water and that of the residents, their furniture, and other items must be calculated precisely.

Although this house boat is essentially a ship, no tradeoffs were made on the interior design. "Our clients love the charm of living on the water, but they don't want to live in a trailer," Houwert says. Nothing in this comfortable 197 square meter (2,120-square-foot) ark reminds one of bunks, galleys, tiny storage compartments, or limited head room. Instead, you think you are in a contemporary, furnished house—and you are! The architects are proud of the seamless transition between inside and outside provided by the white plastered walls that follow the curves of the floating body.

The sliding doors that divide the rooms maintain a boat-like aesthetic, although the entire ensemble, with its glass front facing the water, looks more like a penthouse. Its windows—the frames are made from aluminum like the house's cladding—reach from floor to ceiling so that the nature-loving owners can enjoy the outdoors in all seasons.

The architects succeeded in fitting two levels into their design. Despite the fact that a house boat in Amsterdam is limited to a height of 3 meters (10 feet) from the waterline, you can stand upright on both levels. The architects agreed that this was the greatest challenge. Their solution: a curved chassis that leads to the roof terrace—with a bedroom below with a lowered ceiling. Not only did the design remind them of a Porsche, you could actually drive it under a few of Amsterdam's bridges. And the architects point out another advantage: Contrary to conventional homes, this floating system can be moved on short notice without damaging the landscape, making it the ultimate sustainable building.

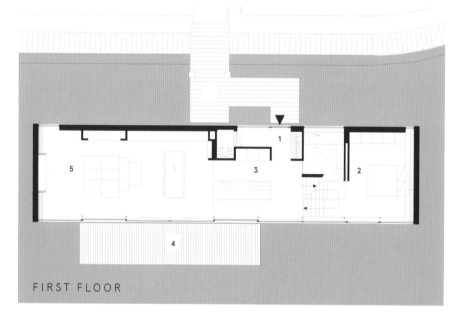

FIRST FLOOR

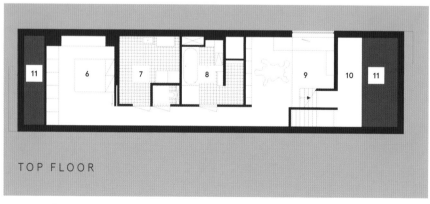

TOP FLOOR

PROJECT DATA

+31 architects
Jasper Suasso de Lima de Prado, Jorrit Houwert

living area: 197 m² (2,120 ft²)
heating:
radiant floors

LEGEND

1 entrance
2 bedroom
3 cooking
4 terrace
5 living
6 guests
7 technical
8 bathroom
9 office
10 storage
11 "box beam"

CONCEPT

Archimedes' principle postulates that a boat weighing 220 tons will only float if it displaces 220 tons of water. Hence the water house was weighed down with additional concrete. It is wider below the waterline to provide extra space and increase its stability. If the width is doubled, as is the case here, the construction becomes eight times more stable.

People have been living on boats in Amsterdam since the seventeenth century.
Here you can live 35 centimeters (1 foot) above the river.
Utilities such as water, gas, and electricity are provided via cables and hoses. A vertical sliding system makes it possible to anchor the house at piers of different height.

SECTION

SITE PLAN

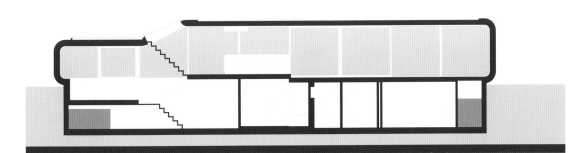

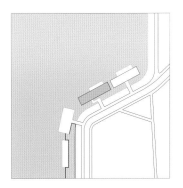

Architects and Photographers

A

+31 ARCHITECTS
Jasper Suasso de Lima de Prado,
Jorrit Houwert
Zeeburgerdijk 209-I
NL-1095 AC Amsterdam
www.plus31architects.com
photographer p. 184–189: Iwan Baan
Photography, Amsterdam, www.iwan.com

ARNOLD/WERNER
Sascha Arnold, Steffen Werner
Seitzstraße 8
D-80538 Munich
Telefon +49 89 189 170 200
Fax +49 89 189 170 299
www.arnoldwerner.com
with Architekturbüro Till Boodevaar
St. Heinricher Straße 18
D-82541 Holzhausen
www.boodevaar.com
photographer p. 66–68: Arnold/Werner,
Munich photographer p. 69: Alexander
Hosch, Munich

B

BARKOW LEIBINGER ARCHITEKTEN
Frank Barkow, Regine Leibinger
design assistant: Michael Bölling,
Markus Bonauer, Annette Wagner,
Philipp Welter
Assistants (completion): Philipp Welter
(project management), André Paaßen,
Verena Schneider
Schillerstraße 94
D-10625 Berlin
www.barkowleibinger.com
photographer p. 92–94: Stefan Müller, Berlin,
www.stefanjosefmueller.de

**BEDAUX DE BROUWER
ARCHITECTEN BV BNA**
Jacques de Brouwer
Dr. Keyzerlaan 2
NL-5051 PB Goirle
www.bedauxdebrouwer.nl
photographer p. 134–137: Luuk Kramer,
Amsterdam,
www.luukkramer.nl

BEMBÉ DELLINGER
Architekten und Stadtplaner GmbH
Felix Bembé, Sebastian Dellinger,
Architekten BDA
Im Schloss
D-86926 Greifenberg
www.bembe-dellinger.de
photographer p. 146–147: Oliver Heissner,
Hamburg, www.oliverheissner.com
photographer p. 144–145: Alexander Hosch,
Munich

C

DAVID CHIPPERFIELD ARCHITECTS LTD
11 York Road
UK-London SE1 7NX
contact architect:
Carlos Seoane, Carlos Fontenla
www.davidchipperfield.co.uk
photographer endpaper, p. 16–23:
Hélène Binet, London, www.helenebinet.com
portrait photo: Christian Kain

**ANTONIO CITTERIO,
PATRICIA VIEL AND PARTNERS**
Via Cerva 4
I-20122 Milan
www.antoniocitterioandpartners.it
photographer p. 138–143: Leo Torri, Milan,
www.leotorri.com
portrait photo p. 190: Wolfgang Scheppe

**CLAESSON KOIVISTO RUNE
ARKITEKTKONTOR AB**
Mårten Claesson, Eero Koivisto, Ola Rune
assistants: Kumi Nakagaki, Patrick Coan
Östgötagatan 50
SE-11664 Stockholm
www.ckr.se
Krakmora Holmar and Drevviken House:
photographer p. 96–101 + p. 124–129: Åke
E:son Lindman, Stockholm, www.
lindmanphotography.com

CORREIA / RAGAZZI ARQUITECTOS
Graça Correia, Roberto Ragazzi
Rua Azavedo Coutinho, 39 - 4 Sala 44
P-4100-100 Porto
www.correiaragazzi.com
photographer p. 110–115: Luís Ferreira Alves
- Fotografia

D

DARLINGTON MEIER ARCHITEKTEN
Mark Darlington, Stephan Meier
Badenerstraße 337
CH-8003 Zurich
www.darlingtonmeier.ch
photographer p. 180–183: Lucas Peters
Photography, Zurich, www.lucas-peters.com

**DELUGAN MEISSL ASSOCIATED
ARCHITECTS**
Mittersteig 13/4
A-1040 Vienna
www.dmaa.at
photographer p. 30–35: Hertha Hurnaus,
Vienna, www.hurnaus.com

E

**ATELIER D'ARCHITECTURE
BRUNO ERPICUM & PARTNERS**
Avenue Baron Albert d'Huart 331

B-1950 Kraainem
www.erpicum.org

photographer p. 70–77: Jean-Luc Laloux,
Anhée, www.laloux.be

F

FANTASTIC NORWAY AS
Håkon Matre Aasarød, Sivilarkitekt MNAL
assistants: Erlend Blakstad Haffner,
Thomas Tysseland, Sigrid Bjørkum
Storgata 37A
NO-0182 Oslo
www.fantasticnorway.no
photographer p. 24–29: Sveinung Bråthen,
Oslo,
www.sbraathen.no

ARCHITEKTEN BDA FUCHS, WACKER
Stephan Fuchs, Thomas Wacker
Am Westkai 9 a
D-70327 Stuttgart
www.fuchswacker.de
www.bigbaybeachhouse.com
photographer p. 36–43: Johannes Vogt,
Mannheim,
www.bau-im-bild.de

G

PETRA GIPP ARKITEKTUR AB
Åsögatan 140
SE-116 24 Stockholm
www.gipparkitektur.se
Katarina Lundeberg
In Praise of Shadows AB
Borgargatan 6
S-11734 Stockholm
photographer p. 162–167: Åke E:son Lindman,
Stockholm, www.lindmanphotography.com

STUDIO GRANDA ARCHITECTS
Smiðjustígur 11b
IS-Reykjavík IS-101
photographer p. 60–65: Sigurgeir
Sigurjónsson, Reykjavík
p. 65 (portrait): Alexander Hosch, Munich

H ——

COOP HIMMELB(L)AU
Wolf D. Prix & Partner ZT GmbH,
Dreibholz & Partner ZT GmbH
project architect: Helmut Holleis
project team: Verena Boyer, Claudia
Buhmann, Volker Gessendorfer, Ana Claudia
Gonzalez, Helmut Holleis, Paul Kath,
Manuela Kaufmann, Volker Kilian, Caroline
Kufferath, Marc Paulin, Sigrid Steinwender,
Irina Zahler, Barbara Zeleny
Spengergasse 37
A-1050 Vienna
www.coop-himmelblau.at
photographer p. 102–107: Gerald Zugmann,
Vienna, www.zugmann.com
p. 104 (top), 109: Alexander Hosch, Munich
portrait photo p. 191: Clemens Fabry

**HIRNER & RIEHL ARCHITEKTEN
UND STADTPLANER BDA**
assistant: Matthias Marschner
Holzstraße 7
D-80469 Munich
www.hirnerundriehl.de
photographer p. 50–52, 54, 55: Sabine
Berthold, Munich, www.sabine-berthold-
fotografie.de
p. 53: Siegfried Wameser Fotodesign,
Munich, www.siegfriedwameser.de

STEVEN HOLL ARCHITECTS
450 West 31st Street, 11th floor
USA-New York, NY 10001
www.stevenholl.com
Daeyang House and Gallery, Seoul, South
Korea: Steven Holl (design architect),
JongSeo Lee
(associate in charge), Annette Goderbauer,
Chris McVoy (project advisor), Francesco
Bartoluzzi, Marcus Carter, Nick Gelpi,
Jackie Luk, Fiorenza Matteoni, Rashid Satti,
Dimitra Tsachrelia (project team)
E.rae Architects: Inho Lee, Minhee Chung,
Hyongil Kim (local architects)

photographer p. 78–83: Iwan Baan
Photography.
Amsterdam, www.iwan.com

Writing with Light House, Long Island, USA
Steven Holl (design architect), Annette
Goderbauer (project architect), Martin Cox,
Irene Vogt, Christian Wassmann (project team)
photographer p. 120–122, 123 bottom : Andy
Ryan, Cambridge MA, www.andyryan.com
photographer p. 123 top: Paul Warchol Studio.
New York, www.warcholphotography.com
portrait photo p. 191: Mark Heitoff

K ——

**KAUFMANN WIDRIG ARCHITEKTEN
GMBH**
Michael Widrig, Daniel Kaufmann
Schöneggstraße 5
CH-8004 Zurich
photographer p. 56–59: Georg Aerni, Zurich

L ——

LACATON & VASSAL ARCHITECTES
Anna Lacaton, Jean-Philippe Vassal
206, rue La Fayette
F-75010 Paris
www.lacatonvassal.com
photographer p. 168–173: Philippe Ruault,
Nantes,

**STUDIO DANIEL LIBESKIND
ARCHITECT, LLC**
2 Rector Street 19th Floor
USA-New York, NY 10006
www.daniel-libeskind.com
photographer p. 156–161: Bitter Bredt
Fotografie, Berlin, www.bitterbredt.de
portrait photo p. 191: Michael Klinkhamer,
Amsterdam

R ——

**ARCHITEKTURBÜRO
ANTONELLA RUPP GMBH**
Bregenzerstraße 43
A-6900 Bregenz
www.antonellarupp.com
photographer p. 150, 151, 152 bottom, 153,
154–155: Oliver Heissner, Munich
www.oliverheissner.com
photographer p. 2, 148, 152 top
Alexander Haiden, Vienna
www.alexanderhaiden.com

S ——

SCHWARZ & SCHWARZ
Dipl. Architekten SIA
Neumarkt 17
CH-8001 Zurich
www.schwarz-schwarz.ch
photographer p. 44, 47, 49 top: Bruno
Helbing, Zurich, www.helbingfotografie.ch
p. 48, 49 bottom: Thomas Züger, Zurich,
www.zuegerpix.ch, Thomas Züger, Zurich,
www.zuegerpix.ch

T ——

THAM & VIDEGÅRD ARKITEKTER
Bolle Tham & Martin Videgård
team: Bolle Tham, Martin Videgård,
Tove Belfrage, Lukas Thiel
Blekingegatan 46
SE-116 62 Stockholm
www.tvark.se
photographer p. 174–179: Åke E:son Lindman,
Stockholm, www.lindmanphotography.com
portrait photo p. 191: Mikael Olsson

MATTEO THUN & PARTNERS
Via Andrea Appiani 9
I-20121 Milan
www.matteothun.com
photographer p. 84–91: Hiepler Brunier,
Berlin, www.hiepler-brunier.de
portrait photo p. 191: Francesca Lotti, Milan

W ——

WESPI DE MEURON
Markus Wespi, Jérôme de Meuron
Architekten BSA AG
Via G. Branca Masa 9
CH-6578 Caviano
www.wespidemeuron.ch
photographer p. 116–119: Hannes Henz
Architekturfotograf, Zurich, www.
hanneshenz.ch

WMR ARQUITECTOS
Felipe Wedeless, Jorge Manieu, Macarena Rabat
Espoz 4066, Vitacura
Centinela de Matanzas S/N
CL-7a Región
www.wmrarq.cl
Fotograf S.130-133: Sergio Pirrone,
www.sergiopirrone.com

INTRODUCTION
fig. 1, 2, 3, 4, 7, 15: akg images
fig. 9: Zugmann, at Coop Himmelb(l)au
fig. 13: Getty images
fig. 16: drawing Archiv Architekten Domenig
und Wallner ZT GmbH
fig. 5, 6, 8, 10, 11, 12, 14, 17, 18, 22: Alexander
Hosch, Munich
fig. 19, 20: Rasmus Norlander, Stockholm
fig. 21: Sabine Berthold, Munich

DUST JACKET
rear flap: private, fig. rear: Gerhard
Zugmann, Vienna, cover picture: Jean-Luc
Laloux, Anhée

Bibliography

Adam, Peter: *Eileen Gray. Architektin / Designerin* (Eileen Gray. Architect/Designer), Kilchberg/Zurich, 1989.

Ibid., *Eileen Gray – Leben und Werk* (Eileen Gray – Life and Work), Munich, 2009.

Azzi Visentini, Margherita: *Die italienische Villa. Bauten des 15. und 16. Jahrherdets* (The Italian Villa. Buildings from the 15th and 16th Century), Stuttgart, 1997.

Bembé Dellinger Architects: *Bilder und Pläne 1999–2009* (Images and Plans 1999-2009), Vienna/New York, 2011.

Campbell-Lange, Barbara-Ann: *John Lautner*, Cologne, 1999.

Cappellieri, Alba: *Antonio Citterio. Architecture and Design*, Milan, 2008.

Chipperfield, David: *Idea e Realtà* (exhibition catalog Padua 2005), Milan, 2007.

Claassen, Helge: *Palladio. Auf den Spuren einer Legende* (Palladio. On the Tracks of a Legend), Dortmund, 1987.

Claesson Koivisto Rune: *Architecture Design*, Basel, 2007.

Claesson Koivisto Rune: *Illuminated by Wästberg* (exhibition catalog), New York, 2009.

Domenig, Günther: *Steinhaus in Steindorf* (Stone House in Steindorf), Klagenfurt 2002.

Domenig, Günther: *Das Steinhaus* (The Stone House), (exhibition catalog), Vienna, 1988.

El Croquis 108, V 2001, "Steven Holl 1998–2002," Madrid, 2003.

El Croquis 158, 2012, "John Pawson 2006–2011 The Voice of Matter," Madrid, 2012.

Hess, Alan: *Oscar Niemeyer. Häuser* (Oscar Niemeyer. Houses), Munich, 2006.

Ibid., *Frank Lloyd Wright. Häuser* (Frank Lloyd Wright. Houses), Munich, 2006.

Holl, Steven: I"dee und Phänomen" (Idea and Phenomenon, published by *Architekturzentrum Wien*) Vienna/Zurich, 2002.

Holl, Steven: Written in Water, Zurich, 2002.

McDonough, Michael: *Malaparte. Ein Haus wie ich* (Malaparte. A House Like Me", Munich, 1999.

Isozaki, Arata und Ponciroli, Virginia (publisher): *Katsura: The Imperial Villa*, Italian/English, Milan, 2004.

Jencks, Charles: *Le Corbusier and the Continual Revolution in Architecture*, New York, 2000.

Le Corbusier: L'interno del Cabanon. Le Corbusier 1952–Cassina 2006 (exhibition catalog), Milan, 2006.

Leoni, Giovanni: *David Chipperfield*, Milan, 2005.

Linton, Johan: *Out of the Real. The Making of Architecture*. Tham & Videgård Arkitekter, Zurich, 2011.

Mnemonic Cartwheel, *Daniel Libeskind's Studio Weil and the Work of Barbara Weil* (exhibition catalog), Berlin, 2000.

Noever, Peter: *Coop Himmelblau. Beyond the Blue* (exhibition catalog), Vienna, 2007

Palladio, Andrea: *I Quattro Libri dell'Architettura*, Book II, chapter 12. (first published in 1570).

Prix, Wolf D. und Coop Himmelblau: *Get Off Of My Cloud, Texts 1968–2005*, Ostfildern bei Stuttgart, 2006.

Riley, Terence: *The Un-Private House* (exhibition catalog MoMA), New York, 1999

Sauerbruch Hutton. *Colour in Architecture*, Berlin, 2012.

Temel, Robert / Waechter-Boehm, Liesbeth: Delugan Meissl 2, Konzepte, Projekte, Bauten, Band 1 und 2 (Delugan Meissl 2, *Concepts, Projects, Buildings*, Vol 1 and 2), Zurich, 2001.

Thoreau, Henry David: *Walden*, Boston, 1854.

Werner, Frank: Coop Himmelblau. *Covering + Exposing. Die Architektur von Coop Himmelb(l)au* (Coop Himmelblau. Covering + Exposing. The Architecture of Coop Himmelb(l)au) , Basel, Berlin, Boston, 2000.

Archithese 4/91: Eileen Gray oder ein unbekümmerter Umgang mit der Moderne (Eileen Gray or an Unconcerned Approach to Modernism) as well as editions of the magazines *2 G, A+U, Abitare, Architectural Digest* (German and international editions), *Arch+, Architecture d'aujourd'hui, Baumeister, Bauwelt,* Domus und Häuser.

Other Schiffer Books on Related Subjects:

Boathouses: Architecture at the Water's Edge, E. Ashley Rooney, 978-0-7643-3190-9

Houseboats: Aquatic Architecture of Sausalito, Kathy Shaffer, AIA, 978-0-7643-2722-3

International Award Winning Pool, Spas, & Water Environments II, Mary Vail, Joe Vassallo, & Virginia Martino, 978-0-7643-3802-1

Originally published as Traumhaeuser Am Wasser by Georg D. W. Callwey GmbH & Co.KG © 2012

Copyright © 2016 by Schiffer Publishing

Library of Congress Control Number: 2015953202

Published by Schiffer Publishing, Ltd.
4880 Lower Valley Road
Atglen, PA 19310
Phone: (610) 593-1777; Fax: (610) 593-2002
E-mail: Info@schifferbooks.com

Designed by Danielle D. Farmer
Cover design by John Cheek
Translated from the German by Jonee Tiedemann
Type set in Apercu/Leitur/Minion Pro/Helvetica Greek
ISBN: 978-0-7643-4959-1
Printed in China

For our complete selection of fine books on this and related subjects, please visit our website at www.schifferbooks.com. You may also write for a free catalog.

Schiffer Publishing's titles are available at special discounts for bulk purchases for sales promotions or premiums. Special editions, including personalized covers, corporate imprints, and excerpts can be created in large quantities for special needs. For more information, contact the publisher.

We are always looking for people to write books on new and related subjects. If you have an idea for a book, please contact us at proposals@schifferbooks.com.